Harley-Davidson

THE · ULTIMATE · MACHINE

Harley-Davidson

THE · ULTIMATE · MACHINE

CLB 3112

9 8 7 6 5 4 3
Digit on the right indicates the number of
this printing.

Library of Congress Cataloging-in-
Publication Number 93-73959

ISBN 1-56138-406-2

This book was designed and produced by
CLB Publishing, Godalming, Surrey,
England.

Printed in Italy by New Interlitho

Published by Courage Books, an imprint of
Running Press Book Publishers
125 South Twenty-second Street
Philadelphia, PA 19103-4399

To Bronwyn, Harley honey and saddle pal for life

SENIOR COMMISSIONING EDITOR: ANDREW PRESTON

EDITOR: DAVID GIBBON

DESIGNER: PHILIP CLUCAS

TEXT AND CAPTIONS: TOD RAFFERTY

PICTURE RESEARCHER: LEORA KAHN AND
ANDREW PRESTON

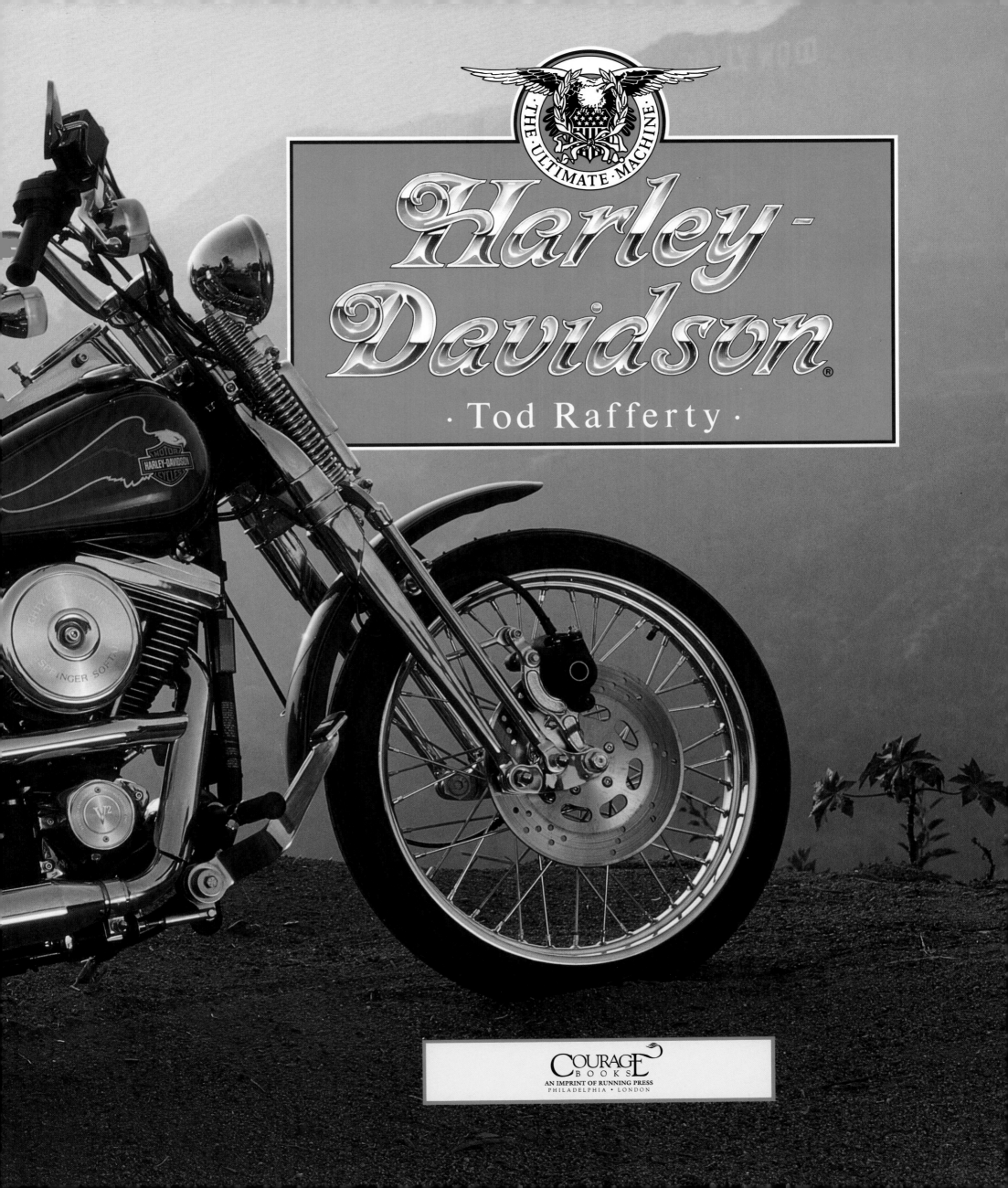

THE ULTIMATE MACHINE

Harley-Davidson

· Tod Rafferty ·

COURAGE
BOOKS

AN IMPRINT OF RUNNING PRESS
PHILADELPHIA · LONDON

CONTENTS

The J model V-twin was a popular choice in the late Teens and early Twenties. This 1920 version, fitted with a sidecar, was the first to have H-D's own electrics.

THE FIRST YEARS

IN THE BEGINNING WAS THE ROAD

AT THE TURN of the century, the American road was more of a path than a highway. European countries had long-established road networks, but the USA was traced by animal paths, horse trails and wagon tracks. And railroads. These routes set the patterns for later roads to follow.

Major cities had streets of brick or cobblestones, but country roads remained largely unpaved well into the new century. Not until 1947 did the mileage of pavement exceed dirt roads in the U.S., and American motorcycling likewise developed differently from its European counterpart.

But roads were only one factor influencing two-wheeled travel. The Puritan ethic called for practical, reliable transportation. Vehicles built for sport seemed a European conceit, not the sort of frivolous activity in which working

Motorcycles found early acceptance in the profession of law enforcement, due in part to the Prohibition Act of 1917. The hot pursuit of moonshiners was part of the job for Officer Friendly.

The 35-cubic-inch (575cc) single, circa 1913, featured chain drive and a two-speed rear hub. The competition for government contracts – military, police and postal services – served to urge a succession of improved machines with each model year. Gearboxes soon got three speeds and a clutch, and brakes were upgraded. Research and development would then get another push with the advent of World War I.

folks should engage. The job at hand was to achieve security through hard labor, not to waste time bashing about on dangerous machines just for the fun of it.

In the 30 years after the Civil War the United States had become the world's foremost industrial nation. The basically agricultural economy was transformed into a society with a growing appetite for manufacturing and mass production. Within its own borders the country had all the elements necessary for industrial expansion; plenty of coal, oil and hydroelectric power. There was a growing supply of labor, eager investors, no trade barriers and a system of canal, river and rail transportation. The industrial revolution was rolling. There was a country to build!

William Harley and Arthur Davidson built their first motorcycle in 1903, the year Orville and Wilbur Wright made their epic motorized flight. The spirit of scientific inquiry and invention seemed to converge with American imagination and enterprise, as the names of Thomas Edison, Alexander Graham Bell and Albert Einstein rose to international prominence. The possibilities were endless.

The American motorcycle industry was already getting crowded by 1903. Dozens of builders were producing machines for sale, most little more than bicycles with makeshift engines. From the group emerged four men who became the forefathers of American motorcycling. Harley and Davidson, of course, and George Hendee and Oscar Hedstrom of Indian motorcycles. A fifth man, who would soon be influential in the fortunes of two-wheeled enterprise, started a car company that year. His name was Henry Ford.

Motorcycles were caused by bicycles. The velocipede obviously needed more speed, without having to pedal. Fortunately for young Harley and Davidson, bicycle chassis

The future of American motorcycling was cast in iron from the beginning. The inlet-over-exhaust valve V-twin was a visible collection of bolts, nuts, rods, levers and springs. A mechanical device, first and foremost, the machine wore its design and engineering for all to see.

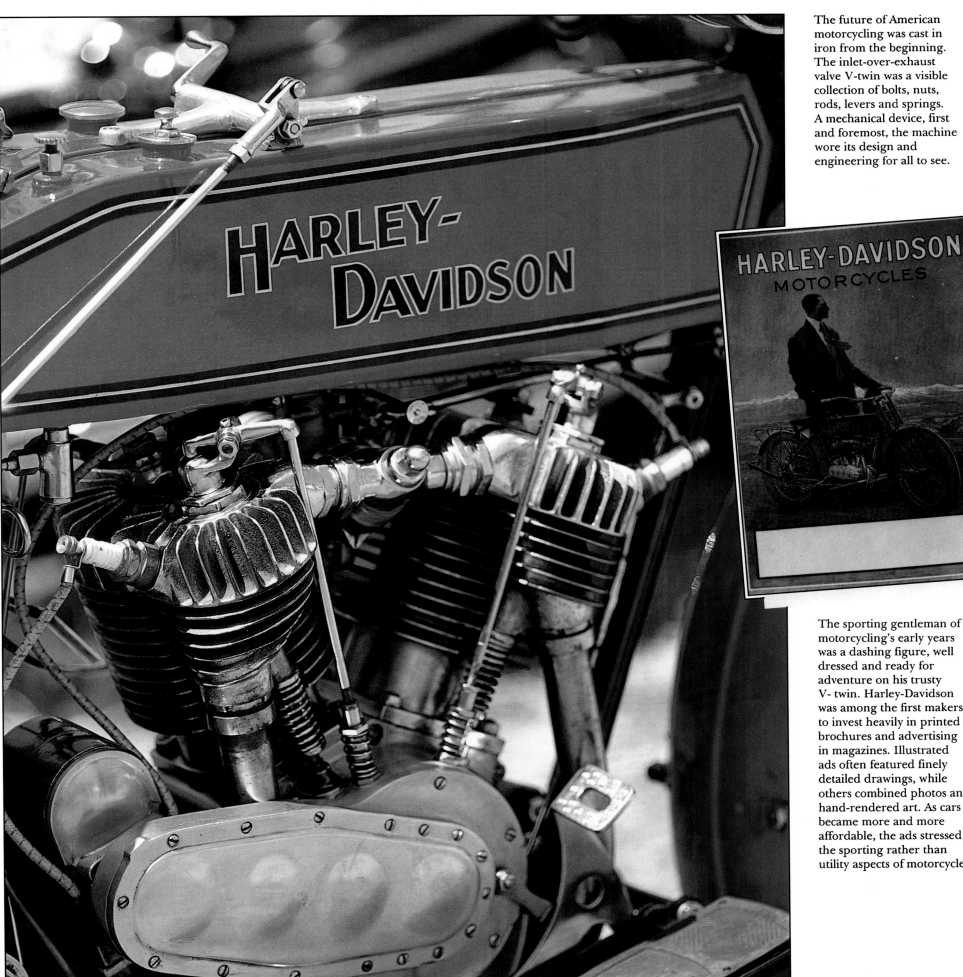

The sporting gentleman of motorcycling's early years was a dashing figure, well dressed and ready for adventure on his trusty V-twin. Harley-Davidson was among the first makers to invest heavily in printed brochures and advertising in magazines. Illustrated ads often featured finely detailed drawings, while others combined photos and hand-rendered art. As cars became more and more affordable, the ads stressed the sporting rather than utility aspects of motorcycles.

development was reaching its apex at the time, just as the internal combustion engine was improving. The marriage was inevitable.

Not all bicyclists were keen on the newfangled machines. Cycling was a serious sport in the 1890s, and professional teams competed for national prizes and glory. Some found the motorcycle merely an affront to gentlemen athletes committed to bicycle competition. "The things are a damnable nuisance," said Boston's Homer Dieble in a newspaper interview. "Popping and sputtering about, belching clouds of smoke. I can't imagine any civilized fellow wanting to be seen on one."

By 1900 the League of American Wheelmen had more than 100,000 members. The "safety" bicycle, perfected in 1885 by Englishman J.K. Starley, had made two-wheeling available to nearly anyone able to walk. And the subsequent

The original home of H-D (**1**) was preserved for many years adjacent to the factory (**3**), but was eventually demolished by mistake.

4: the first Harley-Davidson production model for 1903 and 1904, when three were built in each year. The premier machine drew crowds of fans during the company's 85th anniversary celebration in Milwaukee.

arrival of Irishman John Dunlop's pneumatic tire made it a much less jarring experience. As improvements followed in wheels, gears, bearings and brakes, the modern bicycle quickly reached the configuration it has retained since.

And bicycling also set the stage for the growing roster of speed records that would highlight the first quarter-century of motorcycling. In 1899, Charles Murphy convinced the Long Island Railroad to put 2.5 miles of board track between the rails. Pedaling behind the train, "Mile-a-Minute" Murphy covered a measured mile in just under 57.5 seconds. By then more than a few young dreamers could foresee a way to reach 60 mph with far less effort.

THE SILENT GRAY FELLOW

WILLIAM S. HARLEY was born in 1880 to emigre parents from England. Growing up in Milwaukee, Wisconsin, young Bill enjoyed drawing, fishing and tinkering with things mechanical. His boyhood friend Arthur Davidson shared similar interests, and together they planned a motorcycle. In 1901 both men were employed by the same Milwaukee manufacturing firm, where William was a draftsman and Arthur a pattern maker. With the help of a German mechanic familiar with the De Dion engine widely used in Europe, the new machine began to take shape.

Most of Harley's motorized production (**5**) for 1917 went to the war effort. Hoping to trade on the identity established by its motorcycles, the company introduced a line of bicycles (**2**), but the market was already crowded. The pedal-powered Harleys were too costly and were made for only a few years.

4

The first engine was not a success. But the young men learned that a larger engine and flywheel would be required, and that existing bicycle frames lacked the necessary strength. So they returned to the shop and drawing board. In 1902, with considerable help from friends and the rest of the Davidson family, the first Harley-Davidson production engine was built; bore and stroke were 3.0 x 3.5 inches, with side pocket valves and a larger flywheel. Help on the carburetor design came from Ole Evinrude, soon to be a pioneer in outboard motors.

The elder Davidson brothers, Walter and William A., had both worked for the railroads. Each had the requisite skills – Walter as a mechanic and his brother a toolmaker – to complete a real production team. Persuaded by young Arthur's enthusiasm, and encouraged by their father's blessing on the family enterprise, the brothers signed on. Davidson pere, whose carpentry trade had begun in his native Scotland, built the first Harley-Davidson factory in the back yard. On the door of the 10 x 15-foot shed were

5

By 1915 the machines had developed well beyond the motorized bicycle stage. The market was becoming more sophisticated, and the competition with Indian pushed Harley engineers to develop new motorcycles. The step starter eliminated the chore of pedaling to get the engine running. And the three-speed transmission meant having a suitable gear for the rutted dirt road as well as the open highway.

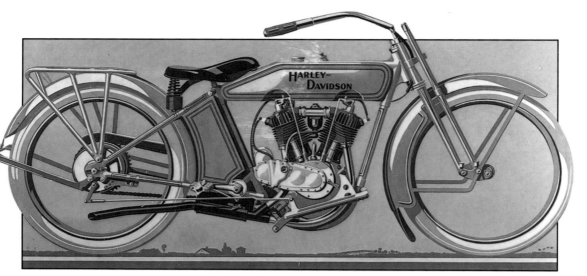

The V-twin, by virtue of the struggle for domination between Indian, Excelsior and Harley-Davidson, was becoming the American engine. Compared to the single, the twin's power output made it much more suitable for use with a sidecar – an important consideration for the young suitor whose mate wouldn't dare ride on the back of a motorcycle.

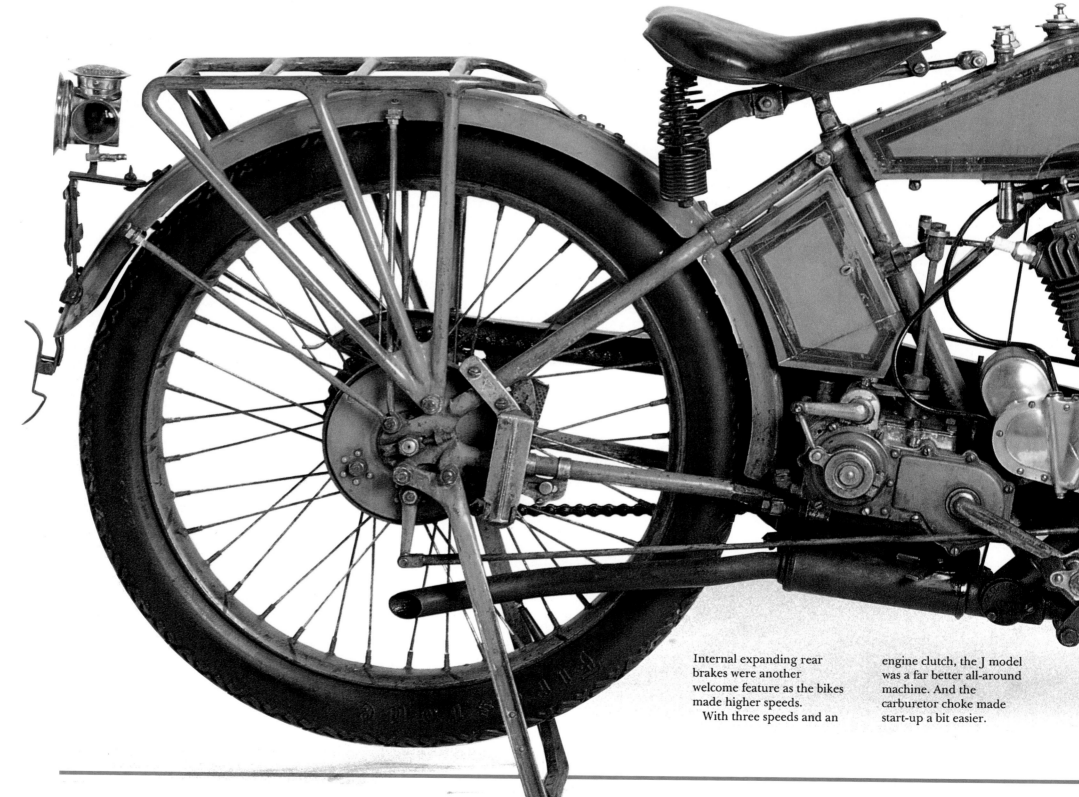

Internal expanding rear brakes were another welcome feature as the bikes made higher speeds.

With three speeds and an engine clutch, the J model was a far better all-around machine. And the carburetor choke made start-up a bit easier.

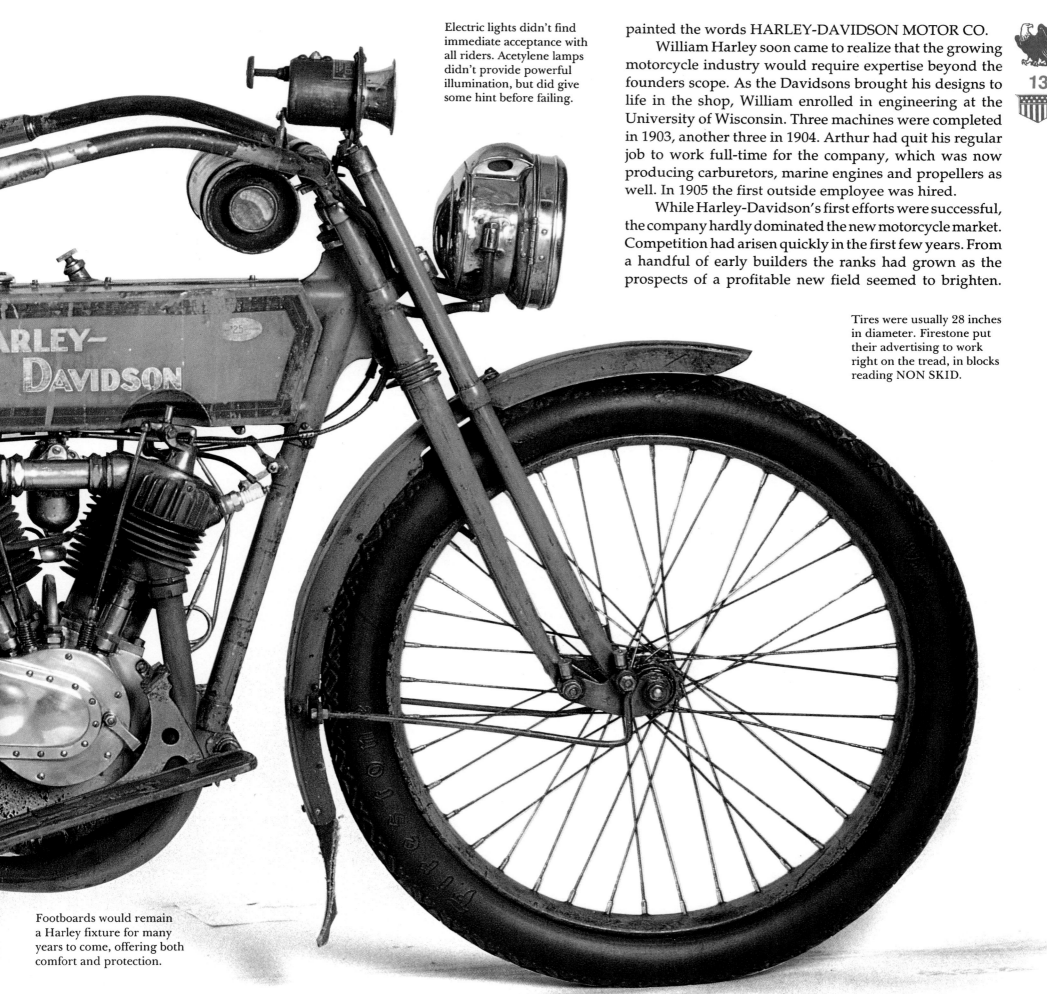

Electric lights didn't find immediate acceptance with all riders. Acetylene lamps didn't provide powerful illumination, but did give some hint before failing.

Footboards would remain a Harley fixture for many years to come, offering both comfort and protection.

painted the words HARLEY-DAVIDSON MOTOR CO.

William Harley soon came to realize that the growing motorcycle industry would require expertise beyond the founders scope. As the Davidsons brought his designs to life in the shop, William enrolled in engineering at the University of Wisconsin. Three machines were completed in 1903, another three in 1904. Arthur had quit his regular job to work full-time for the company, which was now producing carburetors, marine engines and propellers as well. In 1905 the first outside employee was hired.

While Harley-Davidson's first efforts were successful, the company hardly dominated the new motorcycle market. Competition had arisen quickly in the first few years. From a handful of early builders the ranks had grown as the prospects of a profitable new field seemed to brighten.

Tires were usually 28 inches in diameter. Firestone put their advertising to work right on the tread, in blocks reading NON SKID.

1

2

The Harley-Davidson plant (**1**) soon grew to become one of Milwaukee's most modern manufacturing facilities. The founding fathers (**2**) were, left to right, Arthur and Walter Davidson, William Harley and William A. Davidson. Each would leave a lasting imprint on American motorcycling, and a legacy that would endure far beyond their own times.

Merkel, Warwick, Clement, Mitchell, Cleveland, Minerva, Pope, Torpedo, Thor, Pierce, Cyclone, Henderson, Excelsior, Standard and Yale were early competitors.

Automobile prices were still beyond the reach of most middle class Americans, and at $200 the Harley-Davidson was touted as reliable transportation. The general economy was prospering and the founders decided to expand production. With a loan from James McLay, a Davidson uncle, the new factory was built on the site that would become the permanent company home. More employees were hired, and in 1906 the production run was 50 motorcycles or "Silent Gray Fellows" as the new ads proclaimed. Excessive noise was obviously an issue from the very beginning, and Harley-Davidson meant to establish itself as a responsible member of the new motoring community.

THE NEW INDIAN WARS

3

EARLY AMERICAN MOTORCYCLE racing was a curious admixture of country fair festivities and daredevil entertainment. The booming industrial cities provided growing crowds of spectators, eager for motorized action. Harley-Davidson chose not to participate. At least not officially.

In 1907 the new factory put out 152 machines, and despite, or because of, a falling stock market and national depression, the founders decided to incorporate. Shares of stock distributed between family members and the 17 employees provided the funds for a yet larger factory. Walter Davidson became the company's first president.

Although conservative by custom and training, the young H-D managers were not blind to the growing popularity and influence of motorcycle racing. Indian (**3**) had set the pace early on, and sporting enthusiasts were becoming a growing segment of the market. Milwaukee (**4** and **5**), nonetheless, entered the competition arena with caution.

4

5

6

The Harley-Davidson Motor Company expanded steadily in its first two decades. Financed by Uncle James (known as the "honey uncle" since he was a beekeeper), factory Number Two was built on the Juneau Avenue site (**6**). When the 2300-square-foot building had been framed, word came that it was too close to the adjacent railroad right of way. So the crew found a few volunteers, picked up the building and moved it back a few feet.

Despite the growing eminence of V-twins, the trusty single remained the working man's machine for many years.

Shorter on power and prestige than its larger brother, the single was also lighter and less expensive to maintain.

The single – in F-head, side-valve and OHV versions – stayed in the Harley line-up into the mid-thirties, and proved itself on road and track.

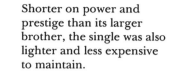

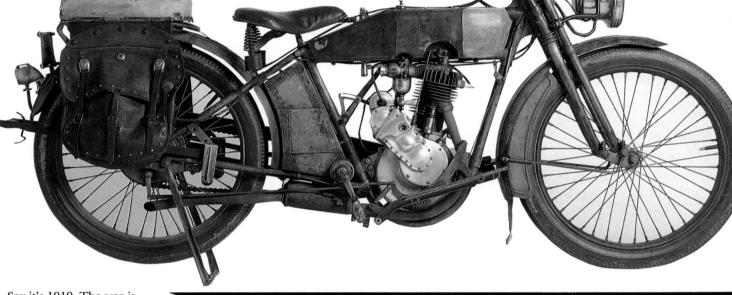

Say it's 1919. The war is over and Good Times are Just Around the Corner. That 1915 model you've been riding for four years is getting a bit frayed at the edges; the engine is still strong, but a paint job is definitely in order. And Harriet always complains about the passenger seat. If you could just get that job down at Muellers, and save up for a new V-twin, wouldn't *that* make Harriet's eyes get big!

Arthur acted as sales manager and secretary, William as factory manager and William Harley was the chief engineer.

By this time the founders had recognized that the growing popularity and market influence of racing could no longer be ignored. George Hendee and Oscar Hedstrom had been committed to competition from the start, and Indian motorcycles were always among the front runners. With like-minded enthusiasts at Excelsior, Thor, Pope and Cyclone, "World Records" were being claimed regularly. The country was moving fast. Faster was better.

Harley-Davidson was a conservative company. The Silent Gray Fellow could hardly be mistaken for a racing machine, being relatively heavy and slow. Durability was the manufacturing credo in Milwaukee; build a strong, dependable machine and the buyer will recognize its merit. Still, the performance claims of their competitors were difficult to ignore. And the company wasn't above touting the results of privateer racers in their corporate advertising:

THE REAL TEST OF A MACHINE
Is in the Private Owners' Hands
And that is where the Harley-Davidson
MAKE GOOD EVERY TIME

Of the founding four, Walter Davidson was the most aggressive, tenacious and the best rider. In 1908 the decision was made that it was time for direct factory participation in competition. Not in a contest of speed and daring, but in the annual Federation of American Motorcyclists (FAM) Endurance Run in the Catskill Mountains of upstate New York. Of the 61 entrants only five rode Harley-Davidsons, Walter among them.

Responding to complaints that previous runs had

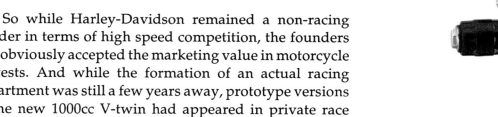

been too easy, the organizers had toughened up the event. The 1745 miles from Catskill to New York City combined gravel and dirt roads, cow trails and water crossings. Special tests were thrown in for surprise and each checkpoint had to be reached exactly on time. In this forerunner of the modern enduro, Walter finished the first day with a perfect score.

For the second day, 190 miles around Long Island, 43 remaining entrants made it to the start line. Again Walter Davidson completed the course with no points lost to win the event. The following week he won an economy run, posting the top mark of 188 miles per gallon. In 1909 the factory entered a four-man team in the endurance run from Cleveland, Ohio, to Indianapolis, Indiana and won the team trophy.

So while Harley-Davidson remained a non-racing builder in terms of high speed competition, the founders had obviously accepted the marketing value in motorcycle contests. And while the formation of an actual racing department was still a few years away, prototype versions of the new 1000cc V-twin had appeared in private race machines as early as 1908.

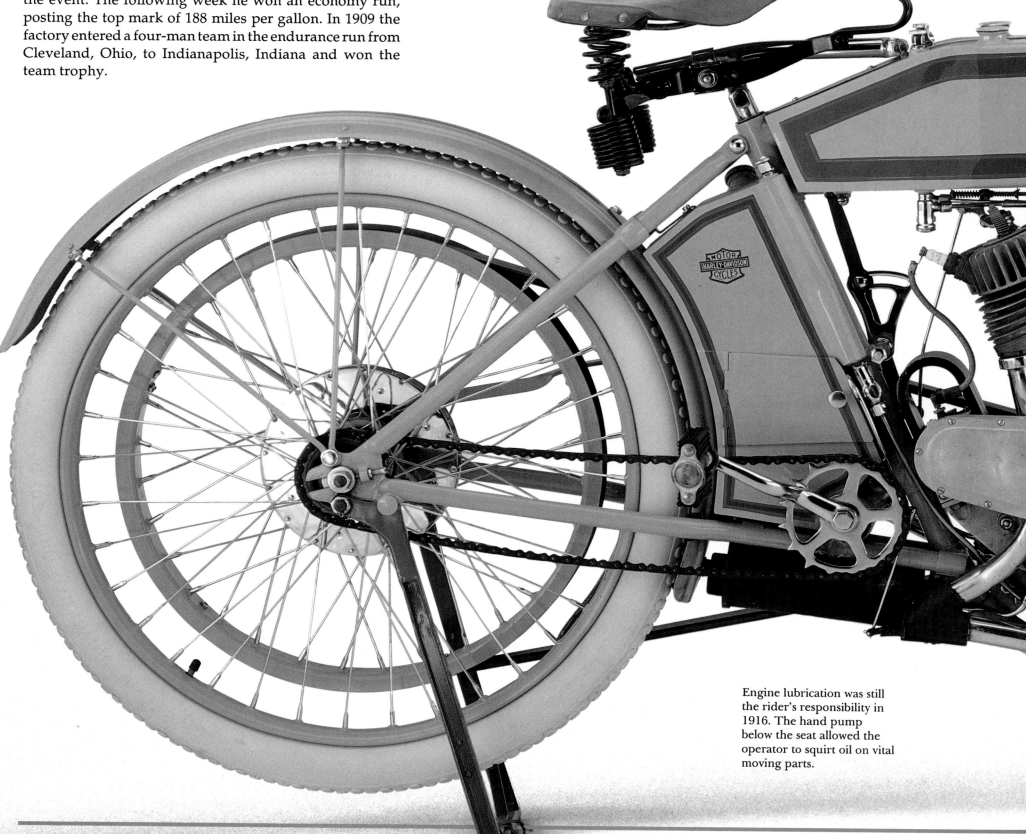

Engine lubrication was still the rider's responsibility in 1916. The hand pump below the seat allowed the operator to squirt oil on vital moving parts.

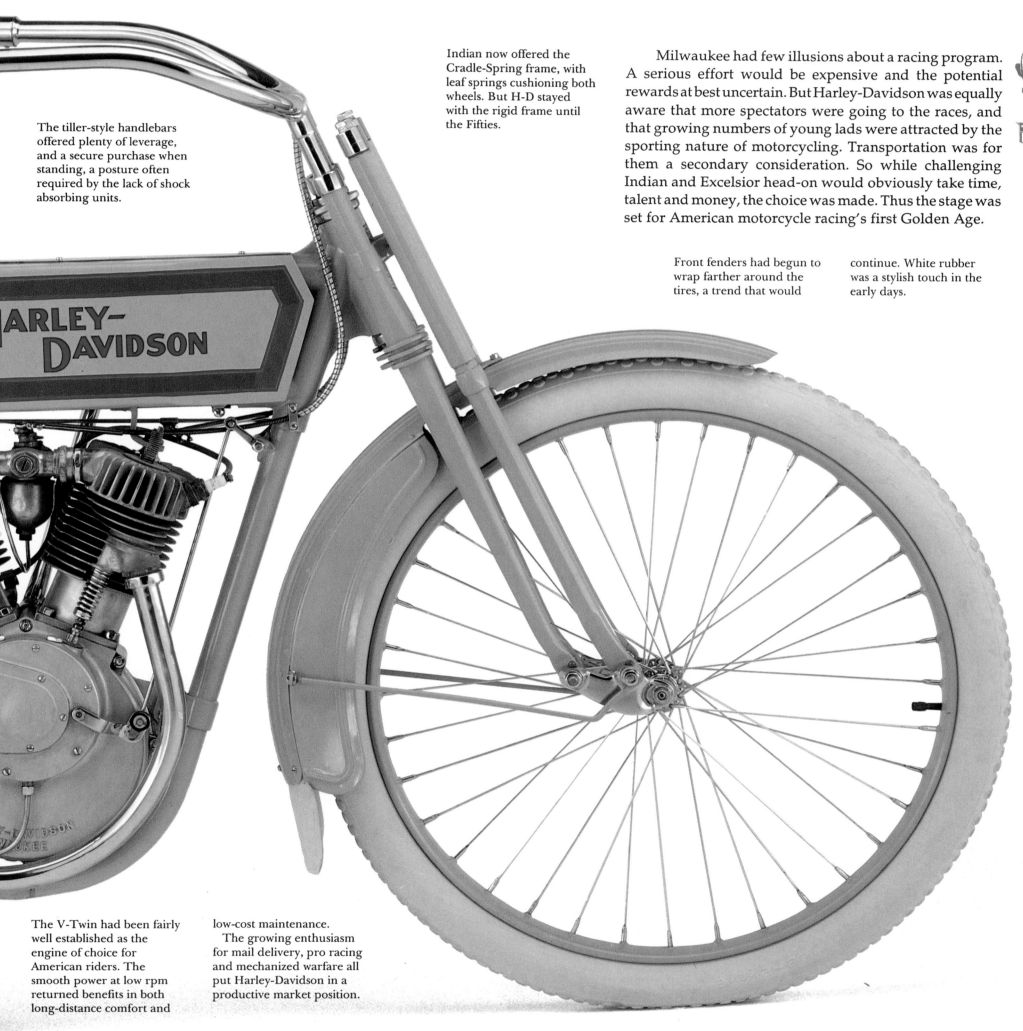

The tiller-style handlebars offered plenty of leverage, and a secure purchase when standing, a posture often required by the lack of shock absorbing units.

Indian now offered the Cradle-Spring frame, with leaf springs cushioning both wheels. But H-D stayed with the rigid frame until the Fifties.

Milwaukee had few illusions about a racing program. A serious effort would be expensive and the potential rewards at best uncertain. But Harley-Davidson was equally aware that more spectators were going to the races, and that growing numbers of young lads were attracted by the sporting nature of motorcycling. Transportation was for them a secondary consideration. So while challenging Indian and Excelsior head-on would obviously take time, talent and money, the choice was made. Thus the stage was set for American motorcycle racing's first Golden Age.

Front fenders had begun to wrap farther around the tires, a trend that would continue. White rubber was a stylish touch in the early days.

The V-Twin had been fairly well established as the engine of choice for American riders. The smooth power at low rpm returned benefits in both long-distance comfort and low-cost maintenance.

The growing enthusiasm for mail delivery, pro racing and mechanized warfare all put Harley-Davidson in a productive market position.

THE AMERICAN RACERS

IT WOULD LAST less than a decade. But American racing established competition standards, for both riders and machines, that were soon to be imprinted around the world. And which locked the U.S. into a staunchly-independent racing framework that would last for nearly 40 years.

The early contests took four basic forms; cross-country, roadracing, board track and dirt track. By far the most popular, and the only one to achieve lasting infamy, was board track. Based on the velodromes popularized by bicycle racers, the motordromes ranged from one-third to half-mile ovals with steeply banked turns. The best circuits were masterpieces of carpentry, with two-by-four inch pine boards laid on edge and banking fitted smoothly into

Early American motorcycle racing was a minimalist affair in terms of protective clothing, as seen in the water-damaged archive print below. Helmets were leather, gloves were often optional. The oil pump handle was within easy reach of the rider's left hand.

The racer's brand identity was clearly established in lettering visible to spectators and photographers. The heavy wool jersey was double thick at the neck, to give some protection from stinging debris thrown up by tires spinning on a dirt track.

the straightaways. As the tracks grew larger and the competition more intense, the speeds increased accordingly, as did the numbers of accidents and fatalities.

Harley-Davidson's first 1000cc V-twin appeared in 1911, and though the formation of a factory racing team was still a few years away, the new machines were soon being modified by private racers. Indian and Excelsior had already spent three years in a running battle for board track laurels, which had accelerated the quest for both more power and reliability.

By 1912 the public outcry over racing carnage had risen in pitch and frequency. The more familiar terms had been changed to *murderdromes* and *murdercycles*. Then, late in the season, a terrible crash occurred at the New Jersey

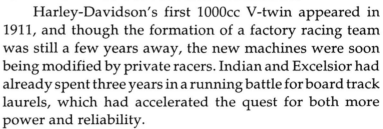

By 1916 the Harley-Davidson racing team, under the direction of William Ottaway, had become a powerhouse. The Wrecking Crew and their eight-valve factory racers brought the challenge to Excelsior and Indian, as racing fans witnessed fierce battles on the popular dirt tracks.

Most circuits were horse racing tracks of half-mile, mile and two-mile lengths. Dust was always a problem, and the brakeless machines would broadside the turns throwing long roostertails of powder. Only the man in front had a clear view ahead.

Around 1916 H-D gave riders the option of belt or chain drive models. Some riders prefered the belts, which imparted a measure of controlled slippage to ease the jolts of the widely spaced power pulses. Better drive-line damping would see chains replace belts, until sixty-five years later, when better belts would supersede chains.

Amateur racers of the era were relegated to riding modified road machines. The daring young man below sports leather chaps and a short-sleeved shirt.

board track killing seven people. The major factories discontinued their support, and American racing was branded by the stigma of the daredevil dromes. The recovery would take years.

Cross-country racing was the exception. One man and one machine blasting across the continent didn't carry the social stain of crazed madmen banging handlebars in a bowl of destruction. A solitary figure, running against the clock and the vagaries of nature; that was a contest with appeal to the pioneer spirit.

Erwin G. "Cannonball" Baker rode tall in the saddle. And the saddle was attached to a 1000cc Indian V-twin, which came to be a source of real aggravation for Walter Davidson.

Baker was the original Iron Man. His stamina was the stuff of legend; he seemed unfazed after riding amazing distances, and covering brutal terrain even in terrible weather. Oscar Hedstrom had built a motorcycle to withstand considerable abuse. It had a gearbox, chain drive, suspension system, kickstarter and removable cylinder heads. In 1914 it represented an integrated, state-of-the-art motorcycle.

The Hendee Manufacturing Company had notified everyone in 1911 that they were more than passing serious about motorcycle racing. At the Isle of Man, in the first year for the demanding mountain course, the Indian team finished 1-2-3 in the Senior TT. That convincing performance was duly noted in a Milwaukee boardroom. Over beer and cigars, plans were in the making.

A few months later Harley-Davidson advertised in *Motorcycle Illustrated:* "No, we don't believe in racing and we don't make a practice of it, but when Harley-Davidson owners win races with their own stock machines hundreds of miles from the factory, we can't help crowing about it."

By this time Harley's market position was fairly secure. Production neared 5,000 machines a year, and orders from

the postal service, military and various commercial fleet operators meant money in the bank. Time to go racing. Confident in their basic design and the machine's strength, Harley-Davidson went looking for a racing tuner.

William Ottaway came on in December, 1913. As design and racing director for Thor Motorcycles, he had established a creditable record. And to Harley's benefit, Ottaway's talents included a keen eye for talent and a gift for efficient team management.

American motorcycle racing now had factory support

from all the major players. After spending 1914 in development and testing, with a few mid-pack finishes in major events, the first Harley Wrecking Crew was ready for the 1915 season. In the 300-miler at Savannah, Georgia, Irving Janke finished third and three more Harleys were among the top eight.

Then Otto Walker and Red Parkhurst put their Harley racers in first and second at the Venice, California, 300-mile event. The clincher came in July at Dodge City, Kansas. Walker won again, and with the exception of an Excelsior

Solo riders disdained the sidecar, but for disabled riders and family men it was pure salvation. The side-van was popular with small companies that offered home delivery.

rider in third, Harley-Davidson riders took six of the first seven spots.

Indian had delivered a powerful serve, and Harley responded with a stinging volley. For two years Harley-Davidson mounted a genuinely-serious racing campaign. Factory riders were equipped with the lighter V-twins with four-valve heads and hemispherical combustion chambers. The FAM required, in the interest of fair play, that specialized racing machines be offered for sale to the public. Harley complied, although the V-twin at $1500 and

the single at $1400 were well beyond the wallets of most privateer racers. Amateurs were encouraged to buy the pocket valve machines at $250, with racing parts as available options.

By 1917 the Wrecking Crew had posted an impressive scoresheet on the boards and in the dirt, and sportsman riders around the country were doing well at hillclimbs, dirt tracks and endurance runs. But racing would shortly cease, with America's entry into World War I. Although competition would resume after the war, and Harley-

The man who could convince his wife that a motorcycle was suitable transport for a family of seven was a living example of American ingenuity. Note the speedometer drive sprocket on the front wheel.

By 1920, nearly twenty percent of the Harley line was being sold overseas, and sidecars made up a sizeable portion of the market. More than 16,000 were manufactured in 1919.

Advertised as Chummy Cars and Pal Cars, the third-wheel machine was Milwaukee's attempt to compete with the ever more affordable automobile.

Comfort, companionship and economy were the combined themes ("40 to 60 miles per gallon!"). And endurance runs and field events usually included a sidecar class. Shown here is a 1918 J model with car.

Davidson's market position would be stronger than ever, other forces would converge to alter the line of racing history.

BEFORE THE TWENTIES ROARED

DURING THAT DECADE-and-a-half in which Harley-Davidson had risen to prominence, the rest of America's transportation industries had moved along as well. Trolleys, trains, trams and buses proliferated, and Henry Ford was gearing up to sell a car to every human being in the country. The French and Germans had taken early leads in auto engineering and production; the names Panhard, Peugot, De Dion, Renault and Daimler were well known. But the automobile was largely reserved for the wealthy in Europe, and no great effort was made to build cars for the masses.

Henry Ford, the farm boy, had little interest in hand-crafted cars for the elite. He meant to build a vehicle that was strong, easy to maintain and cost fairly little. America had strong oil and steel industries, good supplies of rubber tires and plenty of customers ready to buy their first car.

For transportation value, motorcycles simply couldn't compete. The first Model T Ford sold for $850, but within five years the price had dropped by nearly half. For $100 more than a Harley-Davidson V-twin, the traveler could ride inside, warm and dry, not to mention urbane and stylish. Henry Ford had relegated motorcycles to a sporting role in the American motoring mix. Some would come to curse his name, others would express heartfelt thanks.

The Ford effect is reflected in the vehicle registration figures: In 1910 there were nearly a half-million cars on the American roads, such as they were. By 1920 the number was eight million, roughly two-thirds of all the cars in the known world. Harley-Davidson's production for 1920 was about 23,000 motorcycles, which probably included quite some few leftover war models.

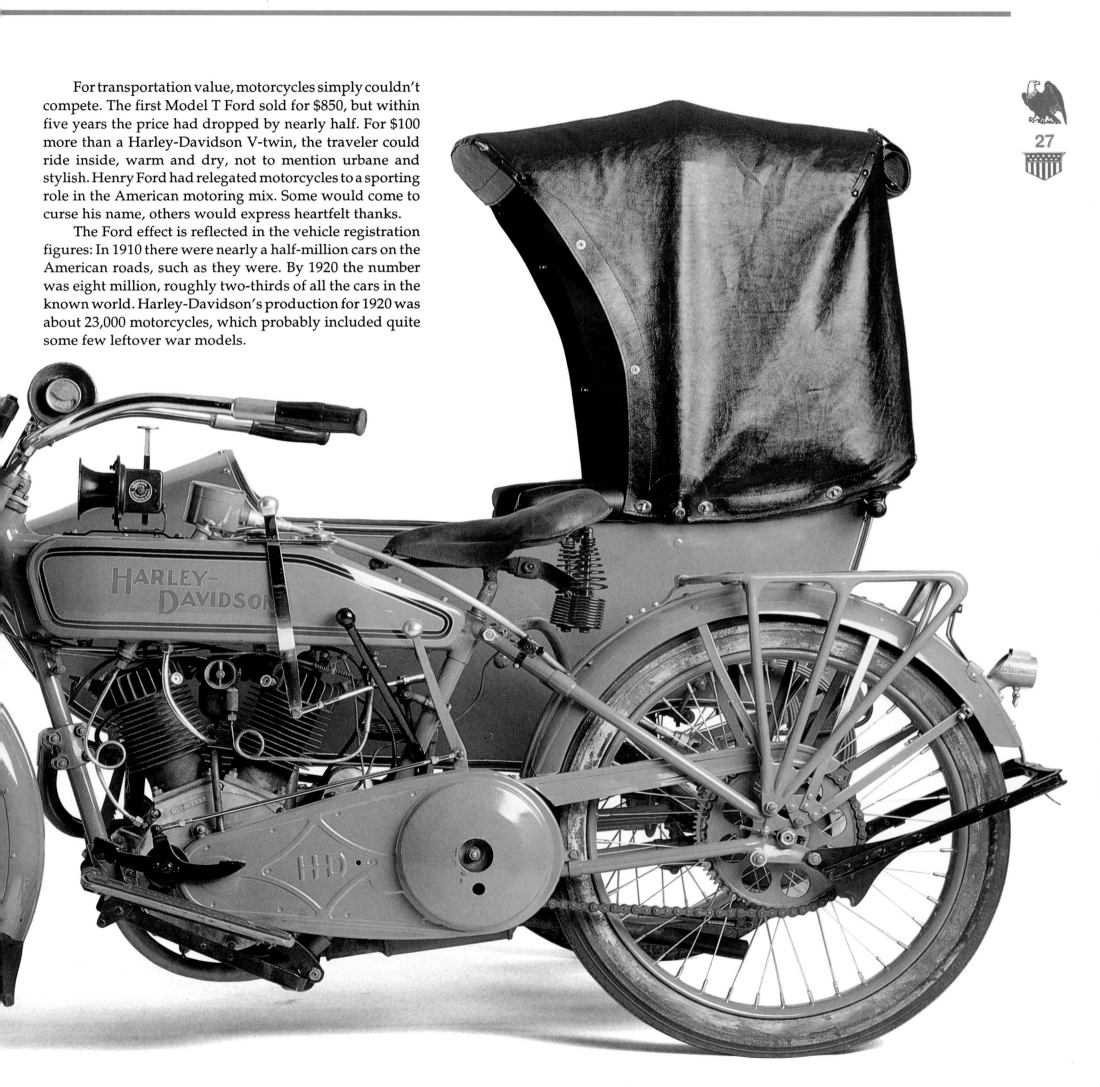

The factory racing effort was suspended with the advent of World War I. By 1918 Milwaukee's total production was devoted to the war effort. Solo and sidecar machines were used by dispatch riders (**1**), and combat scouting rigs were equipped with machine gun mounts. Harley-Davidson began a service school to train soldiers in maintaining and repairing the machines.

Dispatch rider Corporal Roy Holtz was the first American to enter occupied Germany. Twenty-five years later his photo appeared in the H-D *Enthusiast*, where Holtz saw it for the first time.

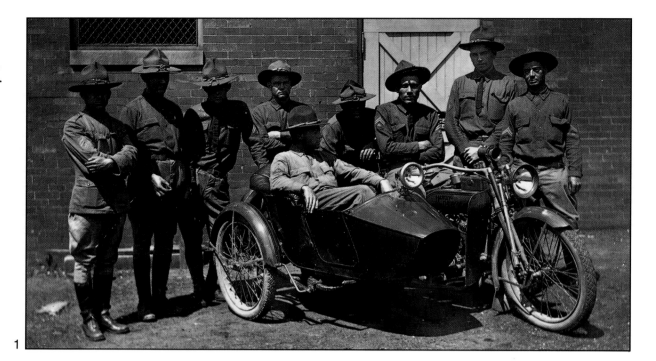

1

In 1919, Harley-Davidson departed from the V-twin orthodoxy with the 37-cubic-inch (600cc) Sport model. The fore-and-aft opposed twin (**3**), patterned after the British Douglas, created little excitement in the market. The Sport was no match for the Indian Scout, and was dropped in 1923.

Racing was resumed after the war (**4**); lining up at the fairground's dirt oval, the lone Indian rider on the left surveys the roster of Harley-mounted competitors.

2

Motorcycle troops (**2**) were first used in 1916 when President Wilson sent General Black Jack Pershing to subdue Pancho Villa in Mexico. The effort was less than successful.

Milwaukee was well-positioned in terms of product after the war, and expectations were tinted with the rosy glow of post-war good cheer. But 1921 was a disastrous year for motorcycle sales. In spite of having dealerships around the world, and retaining the dominant spot in racing, Harley-Davidson was confronted by a drastically diminished market.

PROFESSIONAL RACING, CURIOUSLY enough, continued to flourish despite the tepid market. The FAM dissolved in 1919 and was replaced by the Allied Trades Association, in an industry-controlled group. In 1923 it was supplanted by the American Motorcycle Association (AMA), formed by riders to stress the sporting rather than commercial aspects of racing. As a rider-driven group it lasted only five years,

but established the basis for America's largest sanctioning body.

Racing was forced to change. Economic conditions and increasingly higher speeds combined to re-focus competition rules in the mid-Twenties. Half-mile flat track was limited to 500cc machines, the development of expensive factory racers suspended, and a framework of amateur racing would be levered into place. The 350cc Harley singles, nicknamed the Peashooters, became standard short track machines, while the V-twins ruled the hillclimbs.

Jim Davis was one of the original members of the Harley Wrecking Crew, although he tended to change brands on occasion. "I had a pretty good job with Harley." he recalls. In 1920 he won the July 4 300-mile race at Dodge City. "It was pretty rough on the hard clay. It was about 112 degrees in the shade out there in Kansas, and there wasn't any shade."

Davis won his first big race in Detroit when he was 16. At five-foot-nine and 118 pounds, he had to hear a lot of skinny remarks. "Yeah, someone said that from the front all they could see was the motorcycle comin' at 'em." At the mile board track in Fresno, the bike ahead slung a splinter up that pierced Davis's leather jacket and sunk into his arm. "I didn't even notice it with all the excitement. But after the race, I let loose of the handlebar and my arm stayed folded up."

He liked the board tracks best because they were cleaner, and he liked to dress up. "At Syracuse once I wore a white shirt and a polka-dot bow tie. I changed costumes a lot. They'd go crazy tryin' to keep up with me." Davis rode for whoever he wanted, sometimes got fired and rehired by the same team. He rode for both Indian and Harley-Davidson. "I'll tell ya, they were both good machines.

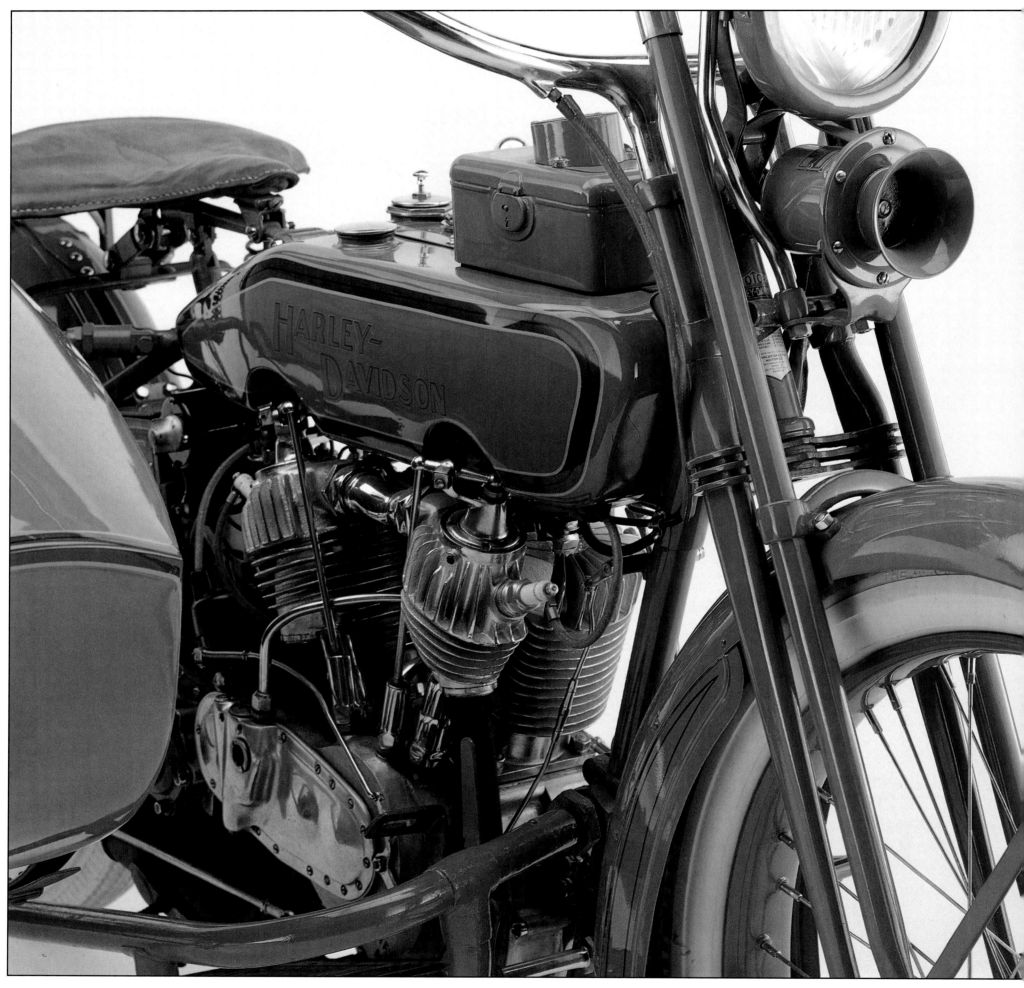

1 and **2**: the 1920 J model with sidecar; a year later the supply of surplus Army green paint would run out.

2

In '26 on the board track at Altoona, I beat the Harleys on an Indian. The next year I rode a Harley and beat the Indians. I'd say it has more to do with the rider than the bike."

In 1990 Jim Davis got married. He was 89.

ARTHUR DAVIDSON AND Bill Harley agreed that new strategies were in order. The bustling moto-market of earlier days was gone, and only two other major contenders remained, Ignaz Schwinn's Excelsior in Chicago and the Indian boys in Springfield, Massachussetts. The primary consideration had now become survival.

Milwaukee turned more attention to the markets that had served them well; sidecars (referred to in some ads as "chummy cars"), parcel cars and motorcycle trucks, with two front wheels holding a cargo box. But motorcycle innovation hadn't been suspended. Recognizing an apparent need for a lighter sport model, Harley introduced the 600cc model W in 1919. The inline opposed twin was a marked departure from traditional Harley design, and despite the compact profile and agile handling, the Sport Model failed to sell. American riders wanted V-twins, and the Indian Scout released a year later sold well.

Henceforth and hereafter, Milwaukee would make no bold strides away from tradition. The public would get what they wanted. And for the next 70 years, with only

Sidecar mania reached its peak in the Twenties. With motorcycle sales suffering under the impact of lower automobile prices, H-D renewed its emphasis on the sidecar as both fun and reliable transportation. Bill Harley and Walter Davidson appeared in the company's ads, inviting the public to test ride the bikes.

The sporting gent of 1922 could escort his sweetheart in style (**3**). They may well be off for the World Series, to see the New York Giants beat the New York Yankees for the second year in a row!

3

minor exceptions, Harley-Davidson staked its existence on the gradual (some would say agonizingly slow) refinement of the big V-twin. And faced with what often appeared to be quite tall odds (many would say insurmountable), they succeeded.

For 1921 the 1000cc V-twin remained the workhorse of the product line. Magazine ads emphasized the benefits of sidecars, usually illustrated with a woman passenger, and underlining the low operating costs as compared to cars. Women had won the right to vote just a year earlier, and the prospect of a new class of independent female riders was an engaging possibility.

THE WOMAN'S OUT-DOOR COMPANION
Gertrude Hoffman owns a
motorcycle – it is the feature-refined
woman-kind
HARLEY DAVIDSON

Below the enticing headlines the copy read: "And many other women are getting the joys of motorcycling

persuading dealers to improve their facilities and cultivate community trust. Magazine ads portrayed the noise-makers as rowdy dolts, and encouraged law-abiding motorcyclists to take action against the offenders. But the nuisance factor had yet to reach a level that would provoke serious effort from any quarter. As the nation edged closer to the Great Depression, the antics of a few hell-raising youngsters didn't make the political agenda.

Both Indian and Harley-Davidson had modified production to meet the military requirements of the war.

Utility was the byword in the Twenties. Harley-Davidson shipped more sidecars, side-vans and parcel cars than ever before. Commercial accounts were critical when sales to the general public dwindled. Gas and electric companies were enticed to use bikes for use by their meter readers.

"Don't use tonnage trucks for poundage delivery," read the ads. "You're carting away profits every trip you take. You're way over your head in overhead. Use a Harley-Davidson."

and the great good of the great-out-o-doors aboard the driver's seat of a Harley-Davidson.

"Motorcycling among women has become accepted as much as horseback riding in days gone by, and the Harley-Davidson responds to the guiding hand of woman as did the kindest tempered steel of old.

"If you are an out-door girl or woman you'll glory in the 'git' and 'go' of motorcycling."

Clever copywriting may have helped Harley-Davidson sustain itself in those troubled times, but other forces worked to degrade the popularity of motorcycles, producing attitudes immune to the persuasions of artists and scribes. Heading the list was the recurrent Image Problem. Already a distinct minority in the transportation mix, riders were ever more aware of the even smaller sub-group that seemed to delight in antagonizing the populace.

More than a few citizens, especially in the cities, came to work up some genuine aggravation over the two-wheeled hooligans. The sudden blast of an unmuffled V-twin easily spooked the few remaining horses on the street, not to mention scaring the infants and elderly. Of course something had to be done.

Nothing much was. Harley-Davidson, as principal member of the Motorcycle and Allied Trades Association, drafted a campaign to upgrade the sport's public image by

Some 30,000 machines went to the allied forces, which did serve as a rigorous testing and research program and provide the cash to put toward new products. With British and European manufacturers crippled by the war, Harley-Davidson was introduced in numerous markets worldwide. In the depleted U.S. market of the Twenties, about 20 percent of Harley's production was exported.

The liberation of the American woman was not overlooked by the Harley advertising department. These ladies are set to ride – the passenger even gets her own handlebar.

NORMALCY AND PROSPERITY

AMERICANS HAD GROWN understandably fond of the pre-war days, when business was good and the outlook cheery. The demand for a quick return to "normalcy" led to the election of Republican Warren G. Harding as president. The banners of conservatism and nationalism flew in the wind, and the post-war celebration began. Having made the world safe for democracy, the time was at hand to get back to the American Way of Life. Taxes came down, tariffs went up and the automobile industry went back into top gear.

This period, known variously as the Roaring Twenties or the Jazz Age, marked the final phase of America's fairly rapid transformation into a global power. The USA now faced its first great chapter of social adjustment since the Civil War. The melting pot was ready to be stirred.

One of the few items unchanged in those changing times was the American motorcycle, which became almost frozen in time. Or at least condemned to evolve piecemeal for the next 25 years.

Harley-Davidson had been stung by the failure of the 600cc Sport Twin. Hopes for the lightweight market were shifted to the 350cc single, in side-valve and OHV form. An improved springer fork was offered on the big twins,

The 61-cubic-inch (1,000cc) J model had evolved over a period of ten years. Milwaukee grew to become a leader in the shaky business of motorcycle manufacturing.

New in '22 was the 74-cubic-inch (1,200cc) J model (**1** and **3**). The Super-powered Twin, rated at 18 horsepower, marked the escalating power struggle with Indian.

1

2

A clean, well-lighted showroom (**2**) could be a lonely outpost in the lean economy of the Twenties.

chrome-vanadium steel came into use, and the teardrop-shaped gas tank reflected the streamlining trend of the era. Even in a diminished market, engineering and designs were now required to stay in the game. And the Springfield bunch kept the Milwaukee lads busy.

Former factory racebikes were sold to European racers. Some Americans emigrated when professional competition dried up in the U.S. Freddy Dixon set a new world record of 106 mph in England in 1923. The previous mark of 103 had been set by Eddie Walker on an Indian three years before.

Pro racing had been demoted by excessive danger on the one hand and shrunken budgets on the other. Class A dirt track was restricted to 350cc engines, and the undisputed king of the class was Joe Petrali of San Francisco. At 16 he had gained attention by finishing second on an Indian against the mighty Harley team at the Fresno board track in 1920. He inherited injured Ralph Hepburn's Harley at the Altoona, Pennsylvania, board track national in 1925. He won the race, clipping almost 14 seconds off the record and becoming the first rider to average over 100 mph. In 1935 he won every mile and half-mile dirt national on the schedule. At Daytona Beach in 1937, Petrali rode the new Harley 1000cc V-twin to a record of 136 mph.

As factory support for track racing evaporated, the cross-country riders again became national heroes of motorsport. The continent itself was still a commanding challenge, and the manufacturers remained open to those with the will and strength to ride 3,000 miles at full chat. Cannonball Baker was still the most famous name among endurance riders, but in 1922 he had a new challenger in Excelsior rider Wells Bennett. Their showdown would feature the respected four-cylinder machine built by William Henderson. The prospect didn't sit well with Walter Davidson, who had tried more than once to sign Baker on

Recognition of the growing movement of independent women came early at H-D. Publicity photos were staged to illustrate females as not only solo riders, but equally capable at the controls of a sidecar rig – her fellow seated in the car. The percentage of women riders did rise considerably in the Twenties, but would later decline as motorcycling became less socially responsible. In the Forties, and also in the Eighties, more women were again attracted to bikes.

for Milwaukee. But Davidson was unwilling to meet Baker's appearance fee, and the champion wouldn't sign otherwise.

Davidson was also worried that Excelsior, manufacturer of the Henderson Deluxe, would threaten the Milwaukee domination of the police bike market, a prime revenue source in a flattened market. The inline fours were smooth and fast, prime selling points for officers who had to spend long hours in the saddle, chasing bootleggers in Buicks.

According to one story, when Wells Bennett was attempting a north-south record in the 3 Flags Run (Canada/ USA/Mexico) in 1921, he was detained for speeding in Fresno, California. After posting his bail the Excelsior rider sped south, only to be stopped by the Bakersfield police

37

Orders for military machines had stopped with the end of the war, but the peacetime army still used motorcycles in training exercises. Hundreds of mechanics and instructors attended the Milwaukee service school during the war, many remaining riding enthusiasts thereafter.

Young men eager to learn the motorcycle business were naturally keen to see how things worked at Harley-Davidson. Although racing at the factory level was suspended by the ailing economy of the mid-Twenties, the chance to see real race machines up close was a rare treat. Factory trained mechanics could count on a measure of job security, as hard times forced riders to keep aging machines on the road for longer periods. And having a fashionable *chapeau* was obviously a social necessity!

Employees of the Buffalo, New York, Department of Health, must have been pleased to make their rounds by motorcycle, despite their rather solemn expressions. Late fall in upstate New York can be rather chilly, and the lads may have been less than eager to ride down to the meat packing plant for an inspection of the refrigeration facility.

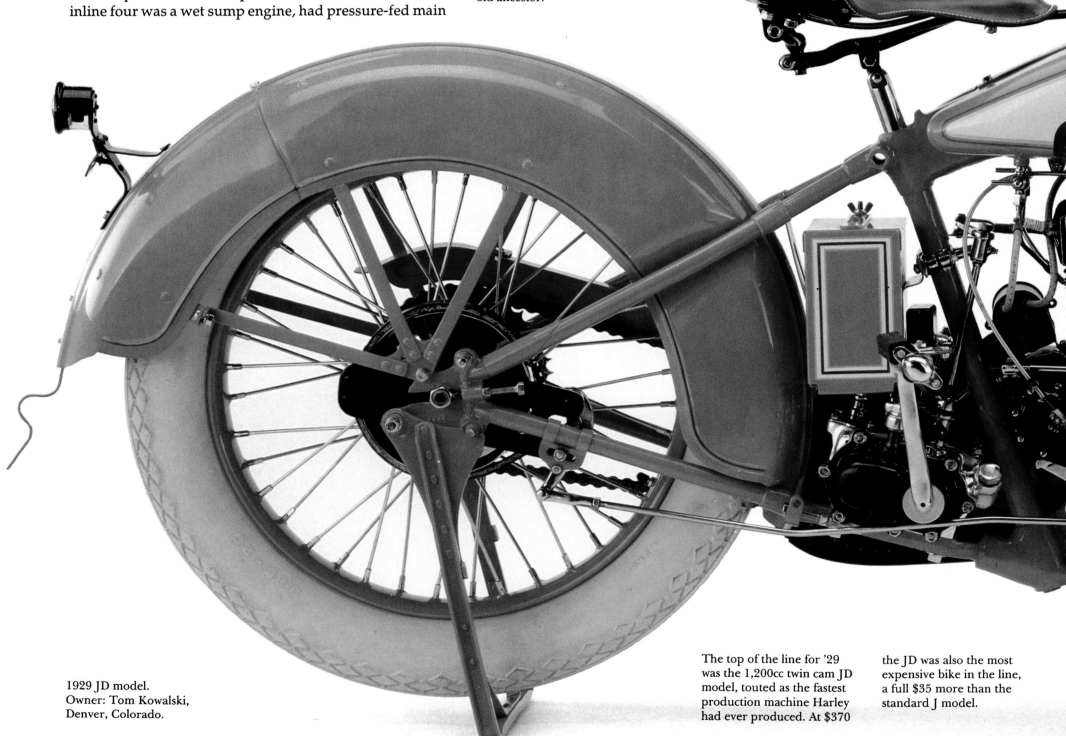

and jailed for the night. Rumor has it that Harley-Davidson dealers had notified the local authorities to be on the lookout for a speeding motorcyclist.

For the Los Angeles – New York dash in 1922, Bennett would ride the Henderson built by Excelsior. The Chicago company was owned by German immigrant Ignaz Schwinn, who had built a thriving bicycle business and a national reputation as a fierce competitor.

Cannonball Baker would ride an Ace four-cylinder, also powered by the Henderson engine. William Henderson had worked with Schwinn's company for two years, but left when his ideas found little acceptance in Chicago. With financial help from another bicycle builder, Max Sladkin of Philadelphia, Henderson produced the ACE. The 1229cc inline four was a wet sump engine, had pressure-fed main

The motorcycle market remained fairly flat in 1929, but the development of new models didn't stop. While Indian, Excelsior and Harley-Davidson took no daring technological leaps into the future, each company continued to refine and upgrade its existing models. The enthusiasts had voted for V-twins, so that's what was built. Experimental models had no role in a sluggish market. The 1929 Harley twin was an updated version of its twenty-year-old ancestor.

bearings and overhead inlet valves, in a bike weighing 365 pounds. Baker galloped across the country in just under seven days, cutting 17 hours off the record.

Bennett's challenge was beset with mechanical problems early on. He made up the time until he met thick fog in Pennsylvania and retired. But he made another run at it a few months later, and eclipsed Baker's time by 7.5 hours.

Despite their engineering and popularity, the fours were unable to survive in the shrinking market. Too few

1929 JD model.
Owner: Tom Kowalski,
Denver, Colorado.

The top of the line for '29 was the 1,200cc twin cam JD model, touted as the fastest production machine Harley had ever produced. At $370 the JD was also the most expensive bike in the line, a full $35 more than the standard J model.

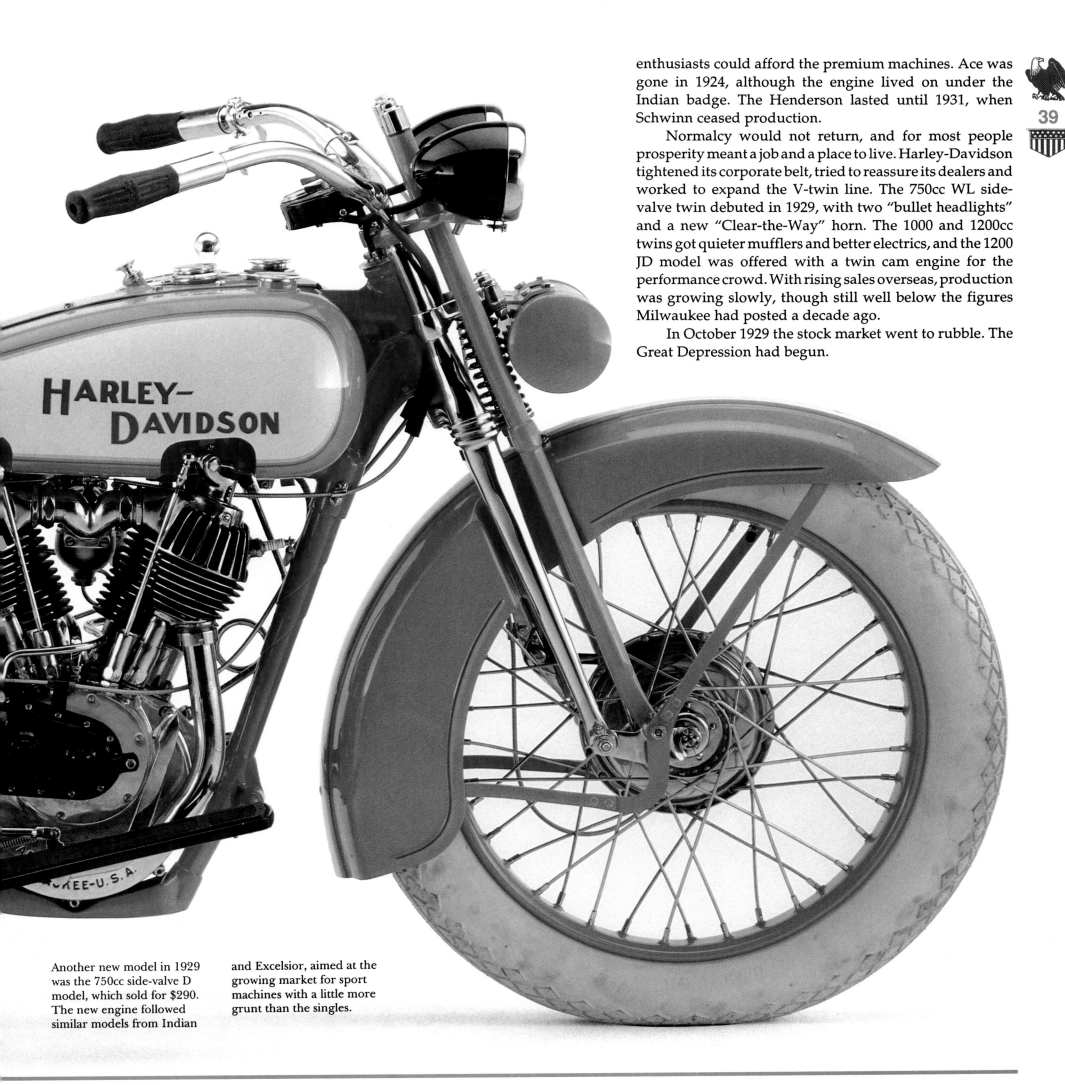

enthusiasts could afford the premium machines. Ace was gone in 1924, although the engine lived on under the Indian badge. The Henderson lasted until 1931, when Schwinn ceased production.

Normalcy would not return, and for most people prosperity meant a job and a place to live. Harley-Davidson tightened its corporate belt, tried to reassure its dealers and worked to expand the V-twin line. The 750cc WL side-valve twin debuted in 1929, with two "bullet headlights" and a new "Clear-the-Way" horn. The 1000 and 1200cc twins got quieter mufflers and better electrics, and the 1200 JD model was offered with a twin cam engine for the performance crowd. With rising sales overseas, production was growing slowly, though still well below the figures Milwaukee had posted a decade ago.

In October 1929 the stock market went to rubble. The Great Depression had begun.

Another new model in 1929 was the 750cc side-valve D model, which sold for $290. The new engine followed similar models from Indian and Excelsior, aimed at the growing market for sport machines with a little more grunt than the singles.

The 1929 JD is an icon marking the end of the classical era in American motorcycling. Its hot rod engine was the ultimate extension of the original V-twin of 1909.

While the JD engine sets it in the past, the future is marked by the streamlined teardrop tank, skirted fenders, front brake and wider tires. The twin "Bullet Headlights," however, didn't achieve lasting popularity.

If any one feature of Milwaukee's farsighted approach stood out in the early years, it was the importance of advertising. Arthur Davidson realized how critical publicity and public relations were to the successful business. That sort of astute foresight, and the commitment to build and back quality products, was to serve Harley-Davidson well in the hard times ahead. And just around the corner was not Prosperity, but the Great Depression.

**1930
1959**

In 1956 only Harley-Davidson was building American
motorcycles, and the 74-
cubic-inch (1,200cc) Panhead
was King of the Road.

THE MIDDLE YEARS

THE THIRTIES

WHATEVER THE ENTERPRISE, glory days are never long-running engagements. They pass quickly into legend or obscurity, preserved only in word, picture and the memories of the original players. The heroes and the villains may grow in stature as the years roll away, enhanced by nostalgia and the rosy lens of retrospect. But gone.

Bill Harley and the Davidson brothers were motorcycling pioneers. In thirty years they had seen the rise and fall of nearly 200 other builders, ridden the economic peaks and valleys, and survived as one of only two motorcycle companies in the country. Each of the four had contributed his own talent and style, and worked the often grueling schedule required for the company's survival.

The Thirties brought more hard times, but the family business was still intact. The sons of William and Walter Davidson joined the ranks, as did Bill Harley's son. Although no startling technical advances were on the horizon, Milwaukee was determined to serve its traditional customers and expand the export market even farther. Agent Alfred Child had organized and developed effective distributors in England and South Africa. In the mid-Twenties he had set up a new sales program for Japan, which soon became a strong market for both motorcycles and sidecars. But the Japanese economy suffered in 1929, and the yen dropped by 50 percent against the dollar, effectively doubling the price of a Harley-Davidson for the Japanese customer.

Field consulted with Sankyo, a Japanese pharmaceutical company, which proposed buying the rights to manufacture Harley-Davidsons in Japan. The founders were more than a bit skeptical about the manufacturing capabilities of the Japanese, but the hard financial facts presented by the global depression worked to influence their decision. For a

Big changes were in store for motorcycles of the Thirties, but that didn't mean the pioneer models would turn into instant relics. Many would serve their riders well for decades to come. "If it ain't broke, don't fix it" became an American axiom. And if it did break, a basic, uncomplicated machine was fixable by the average owner.

royalty fee of $75,000 the Sankyo firm bought the rights to build Milwaukee iron in Japan.

In effect, the first Japanese heavyweight motorcycle was a Harley-Davidson. The new model went on the market in 1935.

The agreement, however, was short lived and Milwaukee broke off the relationship in 1936. Alfred Child became sole importer for Japan, Korea, North China and Manchuria. In 1937 the new Japanese military government imposed an 800 percent tariff increase on imported goods. Child, long a resident in Japan, was politely but firmly informed that he should liquidate his holdings and return to the United States.

With motorcycle sales diminished by the crumpled economy, the development of new models was naturally slowed as well. The JD editions of the Twenties remained the standards of performance until the mid-Thirties and the advent of overhead-valve engines.

45

The 1924 JD was a three-speed hand shifter, with oil and gas caps adjacent on the tank. Just below the gas cap is the oil pump, used at regular intervals for engine lubrication. At the tank's upper right is the priming mechanism, which drew gas from the tank to be squirted into the cylinders for starting. The forward saddle was used by the pilot when carrying a passenger.

1925 JD model.
Owner: Doug Murray,
Stockton, California.

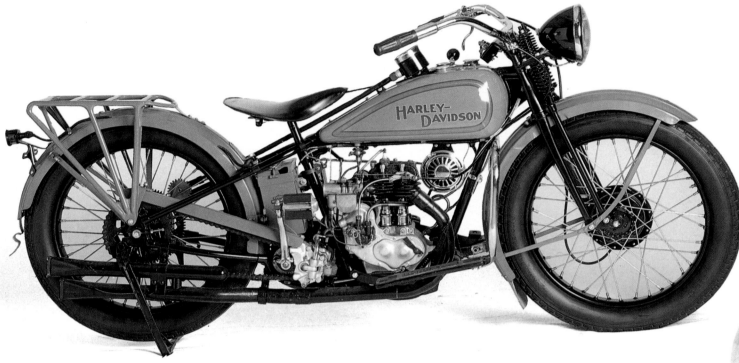

The effects of the depression had reached Milwaukee, and the single cylinder machines would yield to the harsh realities of the economy.

Singles would later return as two-strokes, and again with Italian four-strokes. The V-twin would carry the Made-in-Milwaukee imprint from the mid-Thirties on.

The political relationship between Japan and the USA had been in decline for more than 40 years, beginning with 19th century immigration restrictions imposed by the U.S. government. The long-standing animosity would erupt violently in 1941.

BIKES ABROAD IN PEACE AND WAR

MOTORCYCLING HAD TAKEN different routes in Europe and Great Britain. In countries of smaller geographic scale, with crowded roads, expensive cars and fuel, the big V-twin seemed a solution in search of a problem. Single cylinder machines in both two- and four-stroke designs had become the standard European choice. Most were utilitarian in function, although sport models were available. The Brough and Vincent big twins were virtually hand-made machines for the gentleman sport, and a distinct minority in the overall transportation mix.

Roadracing on the public roads was the popular competition choice early on in Europe, although in England such public displays of tomfoolery were disallowed. The policy led directly to the creation of roadracing's first international showcase venue on the Isle of Man.

American racers regarded their European counterparts with some occasional head-scratching curiosity, but rarely gave it much thought. The Europeans generally perceived the U.S. racing scene with either disdain, disbelief or disinterest, or a combination thereof. So for some 35-odd years there was little racing contact in either direction.

For the USA the harbinger of change, a Manx-mounted Canadian harbinger, appeared without fanfare at Daytona Beach, Florida in 1941. Billy Mathews rode a British Norton 500cc single-cylinder motorcycle and won the race. This event marked the beginning of a new chapter of growing international racing, though postponed by World War II.

The 21-cubic-inch (350cc) side valve single had been in production since 1922, and would survive until 1935. The singles inherited most of the engineering improvements made to the twins, and were offered in 21-cubic-inch (350cc) overhead-valve and 30.5-cubic-inch (500cc) side-valve versions.

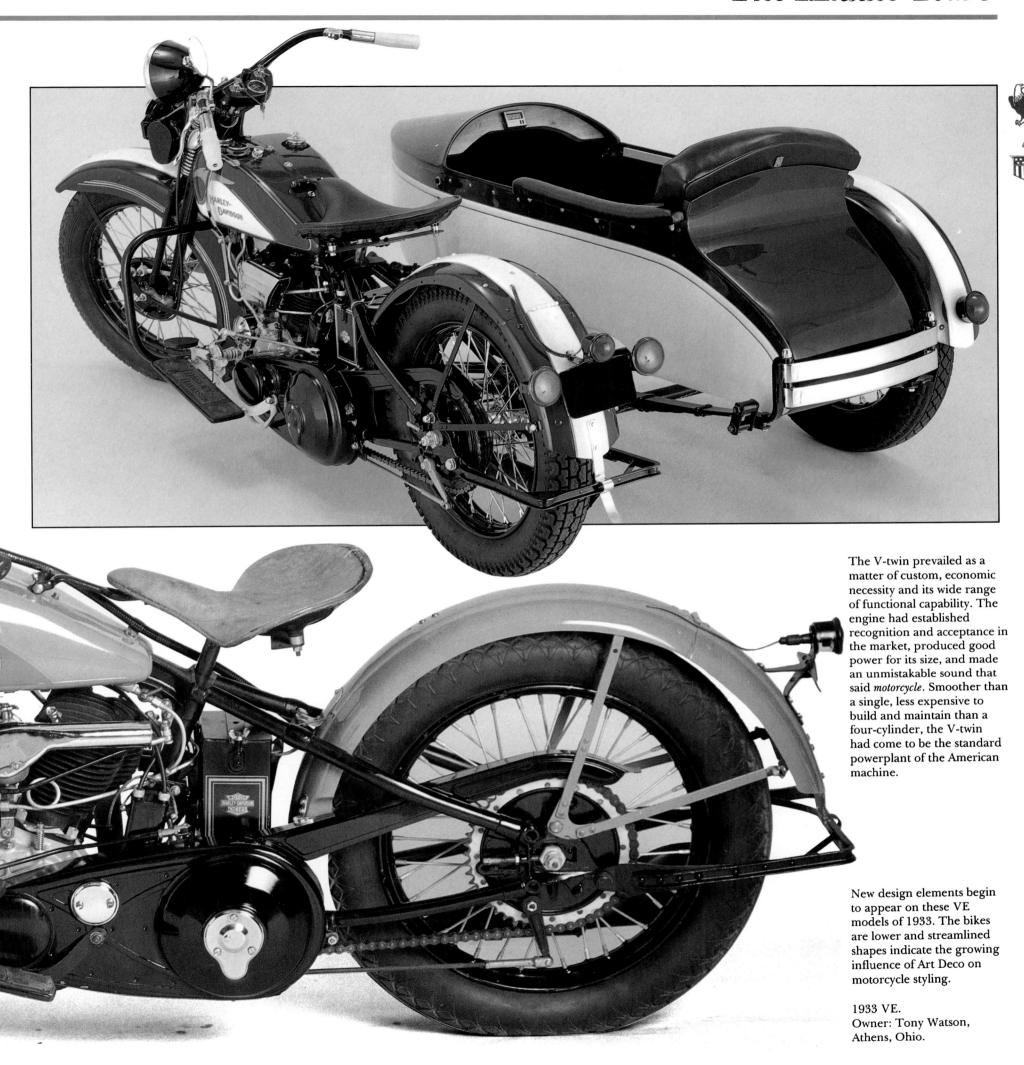

The V-twin prevailed as a matter of custom, economic necessity and its wide range of functional capability. The engine had established recognition and acceptance in the market, produced good power for its size, and made an unmistakable sound that said *motorcycle*. Smoother than a single, less expensive to build and maintain than a four-cylinder, the V-twin had come to be the standard powerplant of the American machine.

New design elements begin to appear on these VE models of 1933. The bikes are lower and streamlined shapes indicate the growing influence of Art Deco on motorcycle styling.

1933 VE.
Owner: Tony Watson,
Athens, Ohio.

The original twin was replaced by the 74-cubic-inch (1200cc) side valve engine, with detachable cylinder heads. The new motor had more compression and higher horsepower, but lubrication remained non-recirculating.

Wheels and tires grew larger, as did the front and rear brakes. The new wheels were interchangeable. The flathead 74 remained for many years the workhorse of the Harley line, the original Hog. The VL/UL series represented the fundamentals of two-wheeled transport, the basic all-purpose machine. For solo or sidecar service, recreation or commercial work, it did the job.

1937 Flathead 74. Owner: Tony Stewart, Malibu, California.

The new influence of styling trends became more apparent in the mid-thirties. The move to decorative art was reflected in not only the tank graphics, but in the elaborate shaping of enclosures for the mechanical bits. Chrome-plated "dashboards" were integrated with the fuel tank. Chromed accessories were offered as options at extra cost. In 1936, Harley proclaimed "New stream-lining, airplane-like in grace. Color combinations that fairly sparkle. The snappiest streamlined sidecar you ever saw." Style had come to Milwaukee.

Harley-Davidson continued their incremental development of the V-twin in the Thirties, while the British and Europeans did likewise with singles. European roadracing champions were national heroes in their home countries. American racing had settled into a dirt track formula to which the narrow, torque-strong twins were perfectly suited. Most of the machines were modified production bikes. The age of barnstorming, pro racing teams had passed into history, and American motorcycle racing was reformed as a fundamentally amateur sport.

But Harley-Davidson's racing budget, although stripped to the bones, never completely dried up. So long as Indian

1933 30.50 single (**1**).
Owner: Richard Davies,
Rosedale, Indiana.

2

The 45-cubic-inch (750cc) flathead (**2**) was introduced in 1929. The economy twin appeared at $290, and would become the little tough guy of the litter. The WL model saw service in the utility Servi-Car, as the WLA military bike, and was the backbone of early Class C dirt track racing. The WR version (dubbed the "Wisconsin Racer") battled the Indian Scout on fair-ground ovals across America.

was in the game, Harley had to be there. The heated battles of the Twenties were not forgotten. Even if it meant selling bikes and parts at cost, Milwaukee would never yield in the righteous struggle to become *the* American motorcycle.

By 1933 production had dropped to 3700 machines, and the single was dropped from the line. The advertising budget was cut to almost nothing and many workers had to be laid off. Without money for mechanical research and development, Milwaukee turned its attention to the appearance of the motorcycle. The shapes and motifs of the French trend in decorative art of the Twenties reached American cars and motorcycles in the Thirties.

The design influence first appeared in the shapes of gas tanks, fenders and instrument panels. Coverings were later fashioned for headlights, brakes, forks and some engine components. The Knucklehead, the 1936 1000cc OHV engine, shows the designer's touch applied to the engineer's creation. The shape of the sidecar was redesigned,

1936 WR.
Owner: "Senator,"
Kewaskum, Wisconsin.

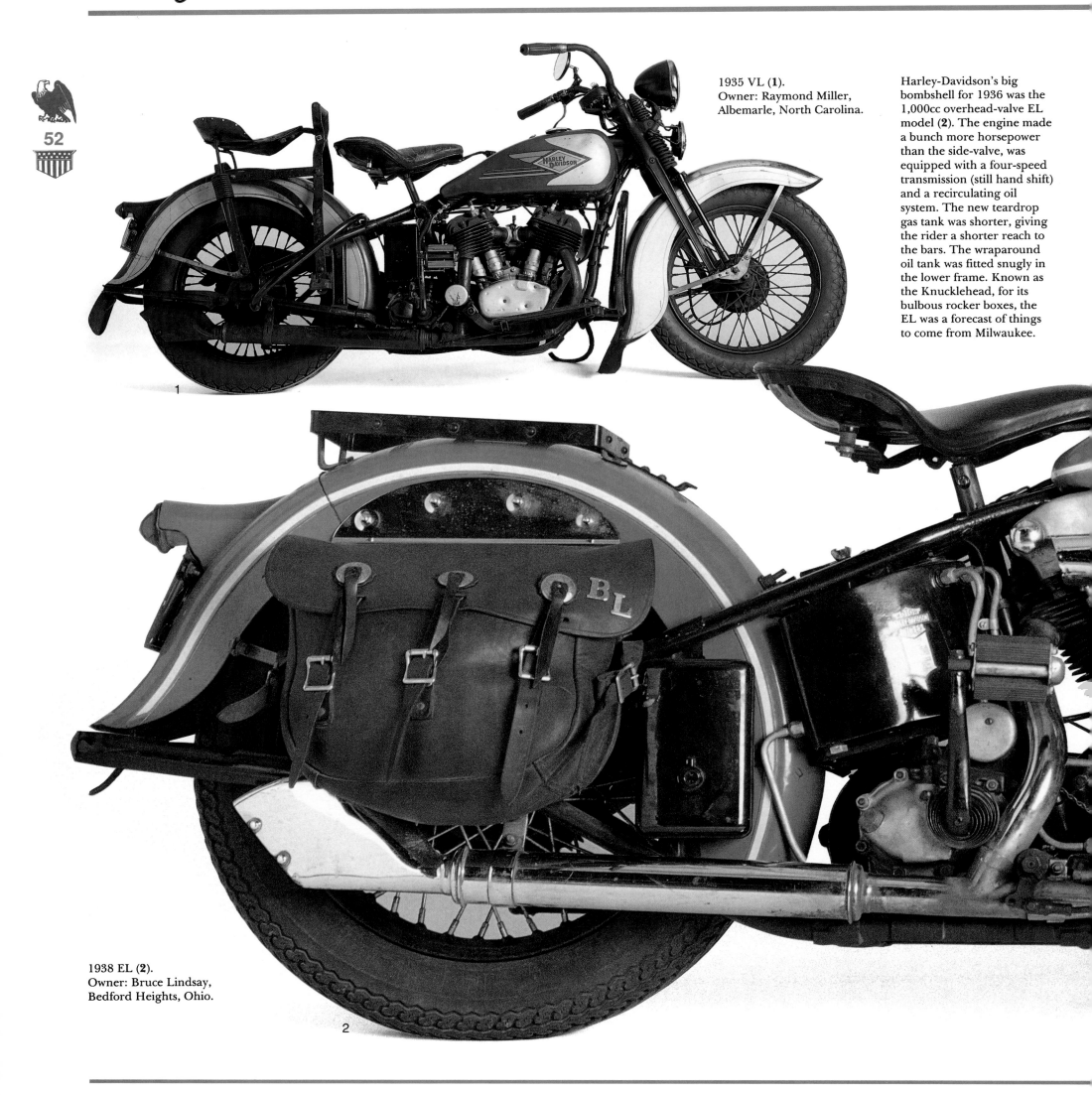

1935 VL (**1**).
Owner: Raymond Miller,
Albemarle, North Carolina.

Harley-Davidson's big bombshell for 1936 was the 1,000cc overhead-valve EL model (**2**). The engine made a bunch more horsepower than the side-valve, was equipped with a four-speed transmission (still hand shift) and a recirculating oil system. The new teardrop gas tank was shorter, giving the rider a shorter reach to the bars. The wraparound oil tank was fitted snugly in the lower frame. Known as the Knucklehead, for its bulbous rocker boxes, the EL was a forecast of things to come from Milwaukee.

1938 EL (**2**).
Owner: Bruce Lindsay,
Bedford Heights, Ohio.

3

An EL (**3**), in its original
livery, is naturally part of
H-D's permanent collection.

With the demise of the singles, the American version of an all-purpose sport machine became the 45-cubic-inch (750cc) V-twin. As professional racing declined, the flatheads became the obvious choice for amateur competition since both Indian and Harley-Davidson built them. Low-budget racers could ride their street bikes to the track, remove the lights and go racing. This was the birth of Class C racing.

By 1940 the 45s had aluminum heads and wore most of the same styling features as the big twins. The WLA military model would soon be in service with the British, Russian and U.S. armed forces.

1940 WL.
Owner: Tom Kowalski, Denver, Colorado.

forsaking the boat bow front end for the modern, streamlined configuration. The focus in motorcycling had shifted from performance to design.

Concurrent with the artistic movement were the New Deal social reform programs of President Franklin Roosevelt. The public works segment initiated bridge and road building on a national scale, which meant more people working, buying motorcycles and riding them on the new roads.

In 1937 works manager William Davidson, eldest of the brothers, died at the age of 66. His son, William H., worked in the factory and had become an accomplished rider, winning the Jack Pine Tour in 1930. In 1942 he would succeed his uncle Walter as president of the company, a title he would hold for 29 years. His son, Willie G. Davidson, would become design director in the Sixties, when Milwaukee would once again look to the designer's pen for marketing help. Or as some have put it, to save its bacon.

THE SECOND WAR OF THE WORLD

ACCORDING TO THE official company history, *The Big Book of Harley-Davidson*, each decade had begun with a renewed sense of optimism.

From a company bulletin: "Supplied with the latest and best in manufacturing equipment, fortified by ample capital, directed by men of vision and long experience, we can confidently draw back the curtain on Harley-Davidson's offering for 1940. In a sweep of the eye we can see that these 1940 Harley-Davidsons are NEW! They are distinct, different, streamlined and breathe the spirit of speed and power."

But for the examples of speed and power displayed by the German army in France, that decade-opening optimism may have been warranted. However, Harley-Davidson wasn't required to convert its plant for the manufacture of weaponry, other than military motorcycles. Russia and Great Britain became primary customers for the 750cc WLA, soon to be joined by the U.S. Army. The jump in defense funding allowed the development of a BMW-style 750cc opposed twin with shaft drive, intended for use in desert warfare. Designated the XA model, it was produced in limited numbers.

The overhead-valve EL had captured the hearts of many enthusiasts who had longed for more power and speed.

Their hopes were certified in 1937 when Joe Petrali set a new speed record of 136 mph at Daytona Beach.

Thunder Chrome: the '41 EL (2) as sparkling musclebike. Owner: Jack Dillingham, Warrensburg, Missouri.

1

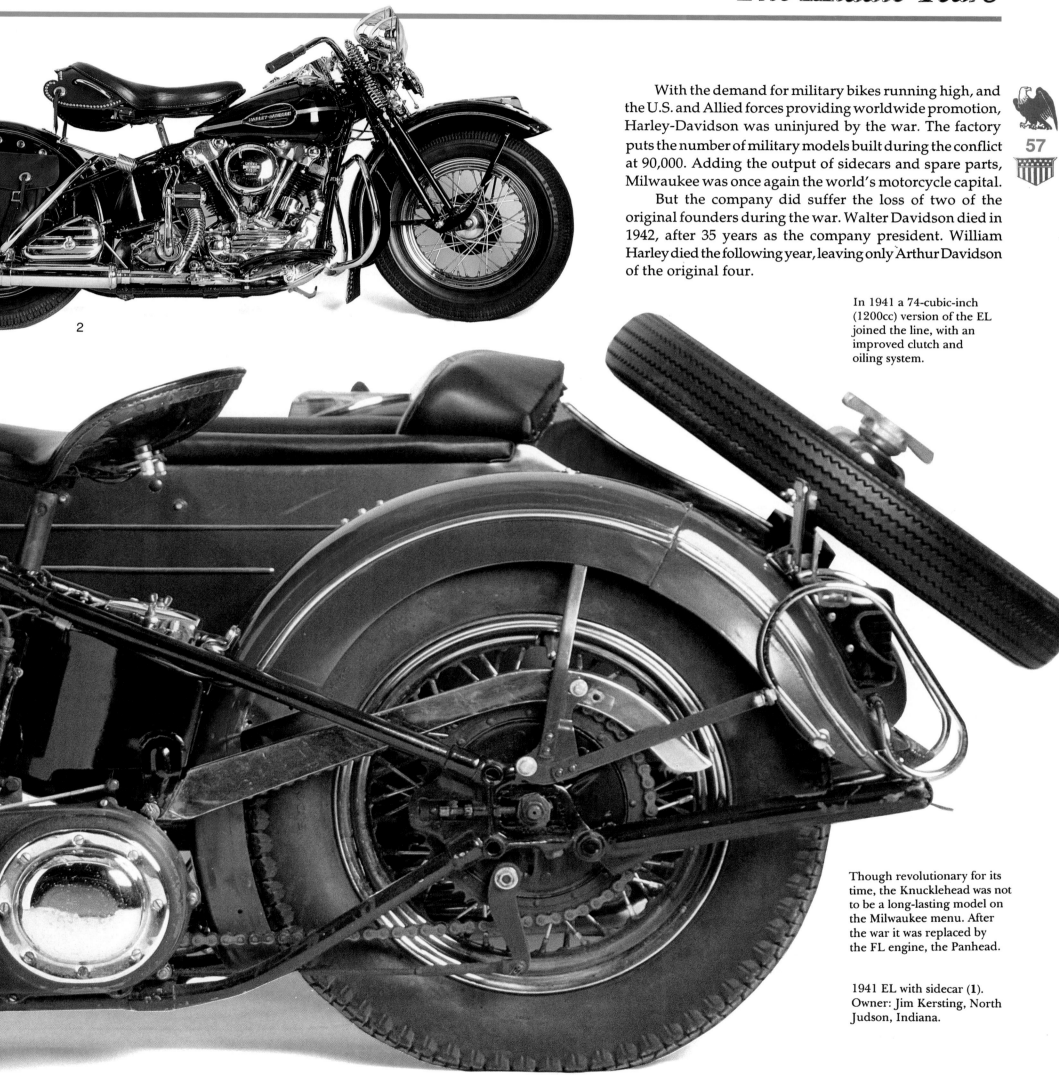

With the demand for military bikes running high, and the U.S. and Allied forces providing worldwide promotion, Harley-Davidson was uninjured by the war. The factory puts the number of military models built during the conflict at 90,000. Adding the output of sidecars and spare parts, Milwaukee was once again the world's motorcycle capital.

But the company did suffer the loss of two of the original founders during the war. Walter Davidson died in 1942, after 35 years as the company president. William Harley died the following year, leaving only Arthur Davidson of the original four.

In 1941 a 74-cubic-inch (1200cc) version of the EL joined the line, with an improved clutch and oiling system.

Though revolutionary for its time, the Knucklehead was not to be a long-lasting model on the Milwaukee menu. After the war it was replaced by the FL engine, the Panhead.

1941 EL with sidecar (**1**). Owner: Jim Kersting, North Judson, Indiana.

2

The economy readjusted slowly after the war, with many materials in short supply and a series of strikes hitting major industries. Harley-Davidson didn't return to full civilian production until 1947, with models little changed from 1941. The clothing and accessories catalog showed more items, including the first appearance of a black leather jacket with chrome snaps, zippered sleeves and belted waist. And with the spoils of war came a Milwaukee version of the German DKW 125cc two-stroke, to serve what was hoped would be a growing post-war demand for lightweights.

Optimism returned for the 1948 season. Guests at the national dealer's conference were taken to a new plant facility just outside Milwaukee, shown the latest 1000 and

World War II expanded the influence of Harley-Davidson in Europe, and introduced motorcycles to many American soldiers who would pursue the sport after the war.

1949 WL (**1** and **3**). Owner: Don Cox, Los Angeles, California.

1200cc OHV Panhead models with aluminum heads and hydraulic lifters, and assured prosperity was on the way.

The official history notes that "seven of the top ten finishers at Daytona rode Harleys" in 1947. Positions one and two, however, went to riders on Indians. The company record continues: "While the races were being won, a certain segment of the riding public began to exhibit some unpopular practices, like using unmuffled engines, weaving in and out of traffic, and cutting up at rallies and events. Perhaps this was due to a release of pent-up post-war energy, or a reflection of the virtually unrestricted motorcycle riding customs of combat – now unleashed on civilian roads. Most notable of these events occurred in Hollister,

Milwaukee suspended production of civilian models in 1942, and H-D devoted its manufacturing strength to the task of building the WLA (2) for military use. Some 90,000 machines were made in the four-year period, many of which were used by the Russian forces. The U.S. Army used motorcycle troops for scout duty, traffic control and dispatch work, as well as a supporting force for armored divisions. Rifle scabbard and saddlebags were standard equipment, as were quieter mufflers. The WL series remained in production after the war. The WR racing engine got more compression, hotter cams and a roller bearing crankshaft. Production-based racing became quite popular in the USA of the late Forties.

The WL engine also saw lasting service in the Servi-Car (4), which had been in production since 1931, and would remain until 1973.

1942 WLA (2).
Owner: Paul Wheeler, Van Nuys, California.

1946 Servi-Car (4).
Owner: Bill Mathis, Moline, Illinois.

California, where the rowdy behavior of a motorcycle group was publicized out of proportion by the national news media. The Hollister event later became the basis for the Marlon Brando movie, *The Wild One*. Incidentally, Brando rode a British motorcycle in the movie."

THE OUTLAW GANGS

"Ever since World War II, California has been strangely plagued by wild men on motorcycles."

from *Hell's Angels* by Hunter S. Thompson.

IT WAS July 4th in Hollister, and the traditional celebration of American independence included dirt track

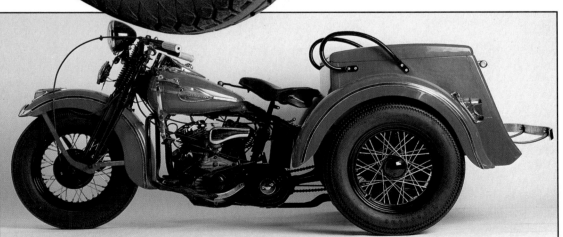

4

Harley-Davidson

60

King of the flatheads was the 80-cubic-incher (1340cc), designated the VLH when introduced in 1936 and becoming the ULH with aluminum heads in 1940. Optional 5.00 x 16-inch tires put more rubber on the road, and ribbed crankcases helped improve cooling.

The big twins found favor with police forces, public service groups and the growing number of motorcycle clubs throughout the country. Many clubs designed elaborate uniforms and emblems to distinguish their groups, and large regional and national rallies grew in number.

racing and a hillclimb. Among the party crowd was a boisterous group of lads who called themselves the "Booze Fighters," who had no connection with the Women's Christian Temperance Union. As luck would have it, a photographer for *Life* magazine was on hand to capture some of the mayhem. Hollywood producer Stanley Kramer later saw the story and recognized the entertainment value in a new feature of American culture. *The Wild One*, was a fictional film chronicle on this new breed of menacing motorheads, which served not only to notify America of the outlaw menace, but to stimulate the growth of the phenomenon it portrayed.

The Bad bad bikers found a hero in Lee Marvin's swaggering hombre (who did ride a Harley), and the Good bad bikers could identify with Marlon Brando's sensitive

adventurer on an existential quest. And sure enough, some of journalism's national pundits would soon cite the film as a *cause* of lawlessness in the streets, if not some devious element in the encroaching tide of the International Communist Conspiracy.

Although the hordes of thundering thugs seldom caused any serious harm or damage unless provoked, there was inevitably one citizen or peace officer for whom their appearance was provocation enough. And with plenty of help from the popular press, the movie became a sort of certification seal that these evil marauders were a threat to society.

The American Motorcycle Association, still closely affiliated with Harley-Davidson, naturally deplored the outrageous behavior of this unsightly "one-percent" of the

The 80-cubic-inch (1340cc) twins were the boss hogs of the highway until they were superseded by the overhead-valve 74-cubic-inch (1200cc) FL series.

The 45-cubic-incher (750cc) would become the longest-running flathead of the Harley line.

1943 ULH.
Owner: Herschel Jones,
Tipp City, Ohio.

motorcycling public. But the image of the cool rebel, in a black leather jacket, had been firmly established in the American consciousness. And it has been recycled every decade since.

But the so-called outlaw gangs wouldn't become a serious inconvenience until the early Sixties. The Late Forties brought Harley-Davidson more immediate concerns in the form of British imports. Aided by the U.S. injection of economic assistance, the British motorcycle industry was back in stride, with lightweight singles and middleweight twins. They featured hand clutches, foot shift, looked nice and didn't cost too much. Harley-Davidson accepted the challenge, in ways not always designed to endear them with dealers or riders.

The Forties and Fifties saw renewed growth in American motorcycling, and the contest for market supremacy had narrowed to the twosome of Indian and Harley-Davidson. Although Indian would fall victim to obstinance and corporate chicanery, failing in 1953, Milwaukee would face yet greater challenges in the form of new machines from abroad. The sport was redefined in the late Fifties and early Sixties, as increasing numbers of sport riders sought lighter and faster equipment.

When Canadian Billy Mathews rode a Norton single to win at Daytona in 1941, most Americans felt it was a fluke. When young Ohioan Dick Klamfoth did it again in 1949, Milwaukee took closer notice. When Mathews won again in '50, and Klamfoth again in '51 and '52, the future had clearly arrived. H-D came to Daytona in 1953 with the new KR model; swingarm frame, telescopic fork and four-speed foot shift.

Paul Goldsmith won on the KR and a new era of American racing, and motorcycling, had begun.

1

2

In the Fifties, another decade begun with renewed optimism, one of the newly-popular two-wheeled runabouts was the Cushman motor scooter. Many Harley-Davidson dealers had added the scooters to their inventory, only to be notified by Milwaukee that it was unacceptable. Pressure was brought on dealers to refuse repair work on imported machines, or even to sell replacement tires to non-Harley riders. Dealers noted the growing number of Triumphs, Ariels and Nortons on the road, and asked when they might expect a middleweight from Milwaukee. They were told it wouldn't be long.

The 750cc K model arrived in 1952, sharing little in common with its ancestor the WL. Though still a side-valve, the engine cases now held the transmission, now shifted by the right foot as opposed to the left hand. It was rated at 30 horsepower but was fairly easily tweaked for considerably more, a note of promise for racers eager to take on the BSA and Norton singles.

In defense of Harley's arm-twisting business tactics, it should be noted that importers were paying only eight

3

1947 EL (**1** and **3**).
Owner: Chuck Todd,
Bakersfield, California.

1947 WLD (**2**).
Owner: Ron Bergan, Leroy,
Minnesota.

The flatheads, both medium and extra large, would deliver reliable service through the Fifties and into the Sixties. But the future was obviously calling for more efficiency and higher performance from internal combustion. Chrome, styling flourishes and colorful paint schemes were not enough to entice many new riders in an increasingly sophisticated market. As the social tempo picked up, H-D put some new life into several aging designs as stopgaps.

1946 WL.
Owners: Robert Beenenga/
Don Fiedler, Tonica, Illinois.

percent duty on foreign machines, while Milwaukee faced 40 percent tariffs overseas. Since the U.S. government had assisted the revival of the British and German motorcycle industries, it could be argued that Washington was encouraging Harley-Davidson's product development by helping their competitors. Curious logic maybe, but the American motorcycle business was rarely accused of rational behavior. And the concept of business and government cooperating for the common good had yet to gain a real foothold in the USA. In fact, quite a few more years elapsed until business owners and their employees began to consider the possibility of cooperation as a capitalist tool.

The popularity of sidecars waned in the Forties. In a healthy economy most folks could afford a car, and the serious motorcycle enthusiast was commited to two wheels. As motorcycling became a recreational activity, the emphasis on practical transportation diminished. The demand for motorcycles was running high as the peacetime economy gained strength, so solo machines naturally had priority in Milwaukee. While the sidecar no longer received the promotional push of past years, enough sidehack fans remained to keep it in the H-D catalog for many years.

1949 EL.
Owner: Les Joseph, Lindenhurst, Illinois.

Those lessons were underway at the time, but the seminars were being held in Japan under the direction of an American named Edwards Deming. An industrial planner and management trainer, Deming was sent as part of another U.S. government program to aid the conquered enemy. His teaching emphasized giving workers more responsibility in the building process, an efficient system to control parts inventory, and methods to achieve and maintain precise quality control.

Forty years later Deming would present the same training to the Ford Motor Company. Shortly thereafter the Harley-Davidson management would see the methods in action, at the American Honda plant in Marysville, Ohio. But back to the painful years in between.

HARLEY-DAVIDSON, APPARENTLY unable to modify its product line to cover new market segments, appealed to Washington for help. Claiming an unfair trade situation, Milwaukee asked the U.S. Tariff Commission for a 40 percent duty on foreign motorcycles and a quota restricting exporters to the numbers they had shipped before the war.

The request met with little sympathy at the federal level. Former Harley export manager Alfred Child, now a BSA distributor, pointed out the company's failure to produce light or middleweight machines, markets which the Europeans had cultivated. He cited Milwaukee's restrictive policies with its dealers, and charged that Harley

1949 125 HD (**2**).
Owner: Ron Magers,
Redford, Michigan.

After the war it was apparent in Milwaukee that lacking a lightweight bike for beginner riders was not good business. Not only would an economic entry-level machine attract new riders, it would help diffuse the rowdies-on-wheels image that had returned to haunt the upright citizens of the sport. At least this was the hope. As fortune would have it, the spoils of war brought the German DKW 125cc two-stroke single. The 170-pound tiddler got 90 miles to the gallon, and looked about as threatening as a bicycle. They called it the Hummer, and it could be yours for $5.50 a week.

was trying to limit the market and drive competitors out of business. The request for higher tariffs was rejected.

So Harley-Davidson continued its traditional pattern of development; dealers were encouraged to form local riding clubs and to promote the growing line of clothing and accessories. The police bike market and commercial three-wheeler accounts remained substantial. Dealers were provided with demonstrator machines for potential customers to test ride.

Arthur Davidson and his wife died in an automobile accident in 1950. As the original marketing force of the company, Arthur was the man most responsible for establishing the national dealer network and the company's service school. His efforts and abilities in both promotion and financing were instrumental in the firm's achievements. With his passing at the age of 69, Harley-Davidson became a second generation family business.

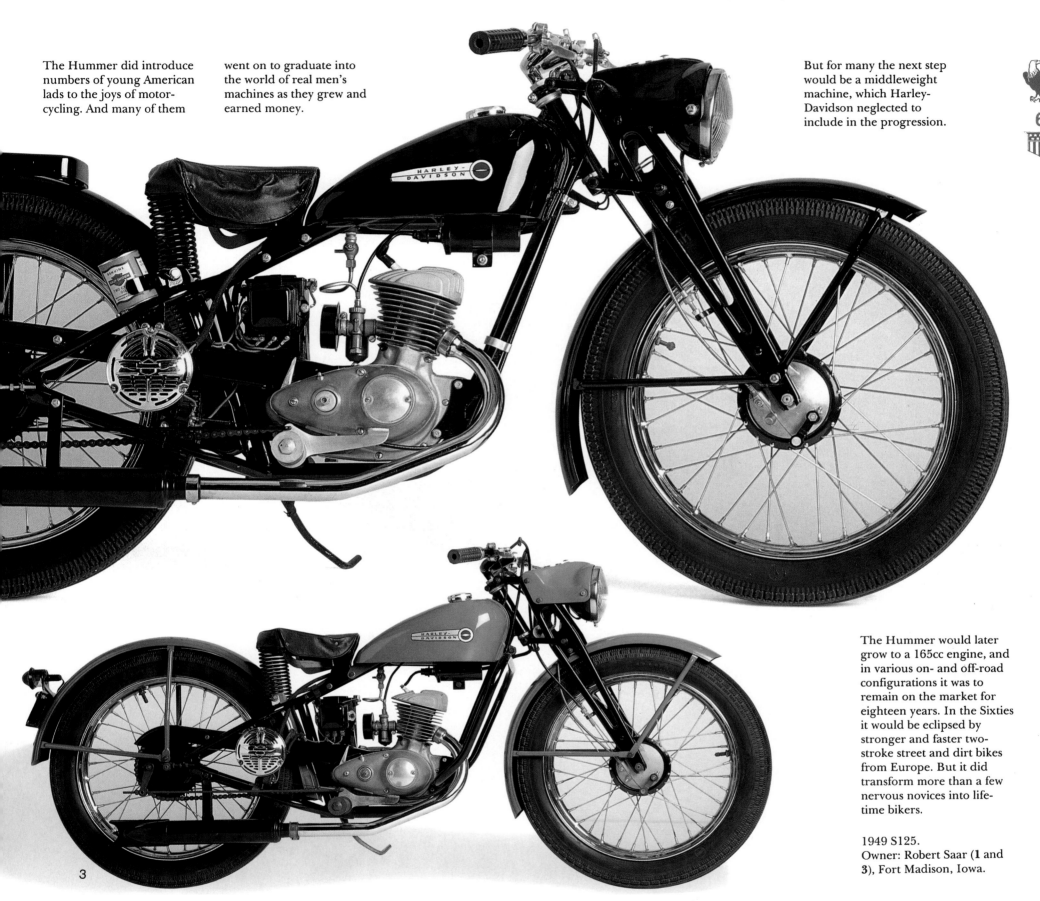

The Hummer did introduce numbers of young American lads to the joys of motor-cycling. And many of them went on to graduate into the world of real men's machines as they grew and earned money.

But for many the next step would be a middleweight machine, which Harley-Davidson neglected to include in the progression.

The Hummer would later grow to a 165cc engine, and in various on- and off-road configurations it was to remain on the market for eighteen years. In the Sixties it would be eclipsed by stronger and faster two-stroke street and dirt bikes from Europe. But it did transform more than a few nervous novices into life-time bikers.

1949 S125.
Owner: Robert Saar (**1** and **3**), Fort Madison, Iowa.

DAYTONA BEACH IS the grandaddy of American motorcycle races. The traditional season opener is the annual showcase for manufacturers, dealers, racers and fans, and an obligatory rite of spring for the winter-weary riders of the northern states.

The race victories in 1947 and '48 had gone to Indian riders Johnny Spiegelhoff and Floyd Emde. Billy Mathews, the '41 winner for Norton, gave Emde a good race and finished second. In 1949 the conviction of Norton's intent was apparent when they appeared with the three-man team of Mathews, Tex Luse and an Ohio rookie named Dick Klamfoth. The young expert won his first Daytona 200, and repeated the feat in 1951 and '52.

The American Motorcycle Association banned overhead

cam engines in 1953. Those were specialized engines, the reasoning went, and American competition was based on production motorcycles. In 1954, following the first through fifth place finishes of BSA riders at Daytona, the Harley-Davidson racing department would come to life once again. This second golden age of American racing would feature the stunning rides of Carroll Resweber, bringing Harley-Davidson four straight national titles. The era would introduce the names Bart Markel, Dick Mann, Cal Rayborn and Gary Nixon, matching machines from BSA, Triumph, Norton and Harley. The history of Harley-Davidson racers, the men and machines, is well covered in a book suitably titled *Harley Racers*, by Allan Girdler.

The Fifties also marked the first technological leaps in many years for Harley-Davidson, most derived from racing activity. Frame geometry, engine placement and suspension systems became matters of experimentation and study. If

The late Forties marked another of motorcycling's major phases of transition. New attitudes and social trends surfaced following the years of war, and young Americans were eager to have some of the things long denied by economic depression and wartime shortages. For the majority that meant a house and car, but a growing faction had eyes for the open road and an unenclosed machine. Sidecar travel was one way to ride and carry the gear for camping and fishing.

"It used to be thought that Harley-Davidson had an unfair advantage in racing because they were running the 750 KRs against the 500cc overhead valve engines. I always felt that if there was any advantage it was the other way around. There was certainly no advantage in trying to race one of Harley-Davidson's air pumps. I thought it would make a great compressor motor, but wasn't worth a damn for anything else.

"In retrospect, I think the Harley-Davidson position was probably correct. At the time, motorcycling was broken up into these almost warring camps. Harley people didn't speak to Indian people, who didn't speak to Triumph riders and so forth. There was a feeling that Harley had undue influence in the sport, because the suppliers also got a vote and there was some politicking of course. They were all Harley suppliers. Even so, Walter Davidson would yank those guys around just by force of personality. He was an inordinately forceful man. And generally he made them do what were good things for the sport. The influence of the AMA may have been out of proportion to Harley-Davidson's real strength, but it was good. There was some good racing between the KRs and the 500s back then."

Gordon Jennings
First WheelBaseman.

Another advantage side-carists had over the solo rider was with public perception. Sidecars were at once cute and practical. The bad guys didn't ride three-wheelers. A group of sidehacks would draw smiles and waves, not frowns and nervous glances.

1948 FLH.
Owner: John Rank, Mequon, Wisconsin.

1

A new fashion trend took hold in the Forties when custom styling spread from cars to motorcycles. The concept of the machine as an expression of individual style created a growing national network of backyard engineers, designers and craftsmen. They used the V-twin as a starting point to assemble motorcycles that were more than the sum of their mechanical components; rolling sculptures that would grab the eye with exaggerated shapes and lines. Motorcycling had a new character in the cast; the tinker as folk artist.

one alteration failed to produce lower lap times, another was tried. And much of the research and development, often the most advanced, came not from the factory but from independent racers and tuners.

Paul Goldsmith retrieved the Daytona trophy for Milwaukee in 1953, the first for the KR 750 and the start of a list of 13 Harley victories there for the following 17 years. The K model set the stage for another span of Harley-Davidson racing glory, dominating the dirt ovals until 1970. And its successor, the XR 750, would carry the flag on into the Nineties.

INDIAN MOTORCYCLES WENT out of production in 1953, leaving Milwaukee without domestic competition but even more crowding from British builders. The vertical twins

New art forms invariably throw the conventional rules out the window. The artisans of iron and chrome were no exception, and the form of the chopped hog was soon a contest for More-Outrageous-than-Thou honors. Beyond a cursory nod to the laws of physics, it was Anything Goes.

1948 Panhead (**1** and **3**), with later wheels, heads, brakes and fork.
Owner: Jerry Parmenter, Des Moines, Iowa.

1948 WR (**1**).
Owner: Brian Haenlien,
Brethren, Michigan.

The girder/spring front fork
had passed through several
upgrades in its thirty-year
history of service. The 1948
model year marked its last
appearance as the
moderator of front wheel
control, replaced by the
hydraulic telescoping fork.
The springer would return,
however, four decades later
in the retro-style age of the
Eighties. Who knows what,
like belt drive, tiller-style
bars and atmospheric valves
may return in the 21st
century?

In 1948 the 61- and 74-
cubic-inch (1000cc and
1200cc) overhead-valve
engines got aluminum heads
and hydraulic valve lifters.
The chromed rocker covers
led to the engine's nickname,
the Panhead. Production
was up and showroom traffic
was on the rise. Happy days
were here again.

The year 1948 also saw the addition of a new manufacturing facility in Milwaukee, which would be used for the production of transmissions and engines.

1948 Panhead (**2**). Owner: Henry Harrison, Hannibal, Missouri.

would grow to 650cc powerplants, with chassis and suspensions winning more fans among American riders who preferred the twisting back roads to the straight line highways. But the Fifties version of high performance remained focused on horsepower and stoplight to stoplight acceleration. Drag racing became the popular measure of motorcycle superiority, and Speed Equipment was widely marketed.

Enter the Harley-Davidson Sportster in 1957. Based on the KH model of only four years earlier, the XL was also an 883cc, four-speed V-twin with the addition of overhead valves. The other significant distinction from its predecessor were the bore and stroke dimensions, respectively larger and shorter than the flathead. The Sportster held a short stroke engine which breathed better, revved higher and held together longer. It was an instant success.

Harley-Davidson celebrated its 50th anniversary in 1953. To commemorate the occasion, the 1954 models received a special medallion for the front fender. The brass logo featured an embossed V enclosing the words – 50 YEARS Harley-Davidson AMERICAN MADE

1

2

3

Even the M165 (**1**) carried the prestigious anniversary medallion in 1954.

MY FIRST RIDE

"My cousin had a '49 Harley with tank shift, and he took me for a ride one night. I didn't know how to ride. A car passes us and the guy blows the horn, and pulls over in front of us and stops. It's a friend of my cousin's, so he goes up and talks for a few minutes and comes back with a big grin on his face. Turns out his friend has two girls in the car, one of whom my cousin has been lusting over. So he wants me to take the bike home.

"I say, 'But I don't know how to ride.' He looks at me for a few seconds and says, 'You're a pretty smart kid, you'll figure it out.' And he leaves.

"It's pitch black, no sound but the crickets, and I really don't know how to ride. I know enough to turn on the ignition and that you have to kick it over. But I don't know where the neutral is, and it's too dark to see the shift quadrant on the tank. So I put it into what I think is neutral, jump on the kickstarter hard as I can, and the thing goes forward off the stand and falls on its side.

"I have a hell of a time picking the bike up. After about three near hernias I get it back, and decide it's time to use my head. So I rock the bike back and forth until I find neutral, jump on the pedal and it spits a few times, but it starts. Then I have to put it in gear, but I can't see where the gears are; but I have a white T-shirt on, so I stand in front of the headlight and enough light reflects off the shirt that I can read the numbers on the quadrant.

"I get back on the bike, and I know the clutch pedal is on the left, but it's on a pivot. No matter which way you push it it stays, and I don't know if you push it forwards or backwards. So I just pick one, try to put it in gear slowly and it goes gggrrrkkgkkgk, so I figure that's not it. Push the clutch the other way, try to put it in gear and it goes ggrrrkkrrrk. So I figure you just have to jam it in, which I do. And it goes thunk, leaps forward and falls over again. Dark … Crickets.

"So I pick it up again, push the clutch the other way and get it into gear. I stall it three times but I get it going along in first gear, and it's about nine miles to my cousin's house, but I figure enough is enough, I'm moving and I'm not going through any shifting stuff. So I ride it back in first gear.

"Finally I pull into the garage, hit the brake and it stalls. So I get off the thing glad it's over, saying 'never again.' That night I'm trying to go to sleep, thinking about how awful it had been, but the more I think about it I realize it might be a lot of fun if I knew how to ride.

"The next day I told my cousin the story, and we went out to a big parking lot and he showed me how to ride. The next year I got my driver's license and my cousin had another Harley, I think it was a '48, and we fixed it up so I could ride with him. That's how I learned to ride. And that's my favorite Harley story."

Paul Dean   Editorial Director, *Cycle World*.

The 74-cubic-inch (1200cc) Panhead became the new king of the road warriors in the Fifties. Its massive Hydra-Glide front fork and deeply skirted fenders bespoke majesty on the open road. As the clear choice for touring riders, the FL reigned uncontested in the heavyweight division.

1951 FL (**3**).
Owner: Dave Royal.

1955 FLE (**4**).
Owners: Rudy & Anna Solis, Los Angeles, California.

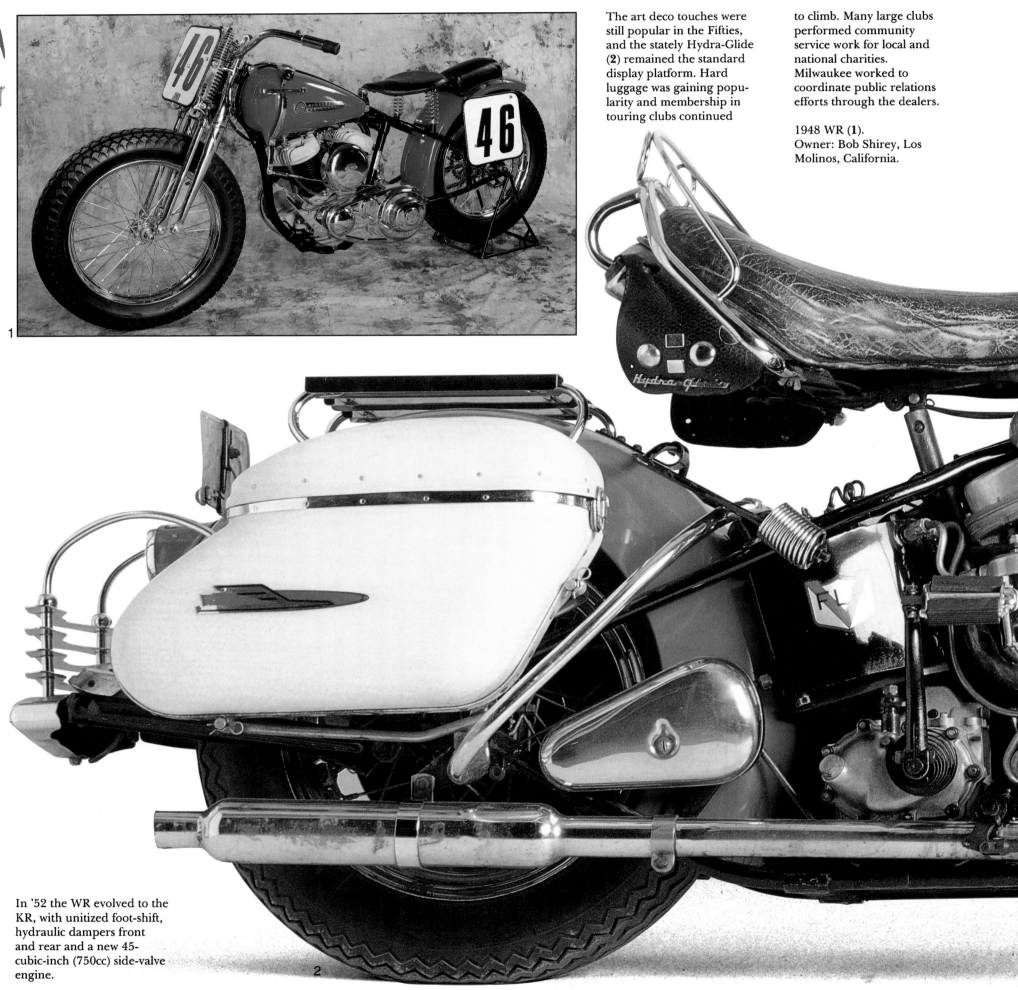

The art deco touches were still popular in the Fifties, and the stately Hydra-Glide (2) remained the standard display platform. Hard luggage was gaining popularity and membership in touring clubs continued to climb. Many large clubs performed community service work for local and national charities. Milwaukee worked to coordinate public relations efforts through the dealers.

1948 WR (1). Owner: Bob Shirey, Los Molinos, California.

In '52 the WR evolved to the KR, with unitized foot-shift, hydraulic dampers front and rear and a new 45-cubic-inch (750cc) side-valve engine.

1956 FLH Hydra-Glide (2).
Owner: Rob Maertz,
Manitowoc, Wisconsin.

The core group of traditional Harley-Davidson customers showed little interest in the Sportster. Why ride a piglet when they could have a hog? The 1200cc Panhead Duo-Glide was the mount of choice for the open road, not only among touring riders and police, but for the growing numbers of chopper enthusiasts. The big twin remained king of the road for carrying a passenger, a load of gear or just looking good.

Those who did embrace the Sportster were of course the younger throttle jockeys, who recognized a hot rod when they saw it. The XL was lean and mean, all muscle and no flab, and it sounded downright nasty. The Sporty was the first salvo in what would become known as the Superbike era, which soon attracted entries from England, Germany and Italy. And a category that eventually enticed the Japanese, who had progressed steadily through the moped phase and were now well into the lightweight/ high horsepower era.

The Harley-Davidson Look was established once and forever in the mid-Fifties. The big twin (74-cubic-inch/1200cc FL) and little twin (55-cubic-inch/883cc XL, ohv version of the KH), would henceforth and hereafter be the permanent Milwaukee duo. Variations that strayed too far from either pattern in form or function would be found unacceptable.

Change would, of course, come to Harley-Davidson, as it did to the country and the world in the next decade. And Milwaukee was to find itself at the precipice of extinction more than once.

Change, in terms of engineering, production and management would become necessary for Harley's survival. But wholesale modification of the Look, the Sound or the Feel, was to be disallowed.

This is the motorcycle we want, was the grassroots sentiment. Make it run better, last longer, shift smoother, stop quicker, whatever. But beyond that, don't mess with it, thanks.

One need only compare the '53 FL with the '93 versions to know that the message was heeded.

1955 FLH.
Owner: Mike Novak, Elwood, Iowa.

80

In 1958 the big twin was granted a swingarm chassis. The Duo-Glide had hydraulic dampers at both wheels, causing some consternation among those devoted to the rigid frame. They saw no need to have *both* wheels bouncing around, not to mention the new-fangled hydraulic rear brake and those whitewall tires. The California Highway Patrol bought a sizeable batch of Duo-Glides, with blackwall tires.

American motorcycling continued its slow but steady development as a buddy sport, well out of the national recreational mainstream. Local collectives of like-minded riders would coalesce around their favorite pastime; weekend road riders, touring groups, dirt trackers and hillclimbers, trail riders and desert racers. Each loosely organized outfit served the needs of its own members, acting as a social club, recreation or competitive sport, or a combination of all three.

More women began taking active roles in motorcycling during the Fifties, following examples set a decade before by the Motor Maids. The popular group of women riders, supported by the AMA, demonstrated that women needn't be only passengers. Dot Robinson, original president of the Motor Maids, became a national ambassador for women riders and was still in the saddle fifty years later.

The market potential of the American scene had captured even more attention among European manufacturers, who

began tailoring more of their production to Yankee tastes; higher handlebars appeared on more imported bikes, softer seats, more chrome and – most significantly – more powerful engines. When increasing numbers of new and considerably improved two-stroke motorcycles began arriving, Harley-Davidson had made the decision to offer a lightweight machine. The process led to the purchase of a half-interest in the Italian firm Aermacchi, which built a 250cc single-cylinder four-stroke.

So Milwaukee entered the Sixties with what appeared to be a fairly comprehensive roster of motorcycles for the expanding market. The Duo-Glide for the heavyweight

1958 Duo-Glide.
Owner: Moon Mullins,
Moore, South Carolina.

segment, the Sportster serving the growing ranks of musclebike fans, the 250 Sprint for the cost-conscious student and sport rider, the 165cc two-stroke Hummer, and even a scooter called the Topper.

IN 1954 THE AMA had revised the national racing format, awarding the Number One plate to the rider winning the most points in a combined series of dirt track and road races. Joe Leonard became the first in a string of Harley riders to become national champion. Brad Andres took the title in 1955 and Leonard repeated in '56 and '57. Then followed the remarkable domination by Carroll Resweber for the Harley-Davidson factory team, winning from 1958 through 1961. Bart Markel kept the title in Milwaukee for 1962.

The spoiler came in 1963, when Dick Mann unseated the Harley powerhouse, taking the championship on a British Matchless. But Harley was back the following year with Roger Reiman topping the points race, and Bart

Markel capturing two more titles in 1965 and '66. Gary Nixon gained the title for Triumph the next two years running, then Mert Lawwill returned the Number One plate to Harley Davidson in 1969.

An adult portion of Harley's racing success in the Fifties and Sixties derived from the direction provided by Dick O'Brien, who took over as team chief in 1957. O'Brien was a race tuner himself, but he brought to the job a range of other talents. Combining the abilities of a master sergeant and a good buddy, O'Brien served as cheerleader, taskmaster, mother hen and final authority. And his teams evolved as a worthy second generation of the original Harley Wrecking Crew.

But, despite their role as sole defender of the American motorcycle industry in the Fifties, the Harley racing team created nary a ripple of interest among the general public.

1

1957 Sportster (**2**).
Owner: Kevin Meyer, Erie,
Illinois.

2

Younger riders on a Hummer (**1**) budget had eyes of envy for the riders of the mighty Sportster.

The 55-cubic-inch (883cc) overhead-valve XL was the lone American entry in what would come to be called the Superbike class. Descended directly from the K model, the new Sportster (**2**) was muscular but trim. No extraneous fixtures were hung on the machine to dilute its hot rod look. Touring and more mundane utility chores were left to the big twins; the designated mission of the Sportster was to haul ass. As a straight-line sprinter, it was the class champ.

Baseball and football remained the top spectator sports, supplemented by the widespread proliferation of a new entertainment device called television. The dominant influences in pop culture were Elvis Presley, Marlon Brando and James Dean. And after a bloody stalemate with the Chinese in Korea, America again looked for the elusive calm of normalcy. And along came rock 'n' roll.

Many a societal current sends ripples far beyond the crest of its initial wave, but the next riptide is then underway down below. Rock 'n' roll, much like the Harley-Davidson Motor Company, would rise from its own ashes more than once. But the product can never be the same as the original, it's a biological impossibility. The difference between Harley-Davidson's comebacks and those of rock 'n' roll is that Harley's products were better than the originals.

IN 1953 THE Motor Company celebrated its 50th anniversary, and William H. Davidson presented the celebration dinner speech. "Harley-Davidson's achievements over

The reign of the Sportster (**2**) as king of the muscle-bound roadsters would not remain unchallenged for long. The British manufacturers had been building a distribution network in the U.S., and the XL was a prime target in the coming showdown for high performance honors.

Speed in the American idiom was fundamentally a matter of straight line acceleration; drop the hammer and see who is fastest from point-to-point. Quarter-mile elapsed time and top speed were the standard measures of high performance.

Europeans, with a long tradition of roadracing, held rather different views of sporting contests. While acceleration and velocity were hardly ignored, the qualities of roadholding and cornering agility were equally important. Chassis and suspension development received more attention in the European sportbike equation. Soon American riders would have more choice.

1

The baby brother of the Harley line, the 165cc two-stroke (**2**), was looking a bit sportier in 1959. The tiddlers would soon be available in 175cc models, but the little bikes had never quite lived up to the market expectations Milwaukee had charted. When domestic production no longer made economic sense, a new line of lightweights would be imported from Italy.

1959 165 (**2**).
Owner: Bob Southwick, East Moline, Illinois.

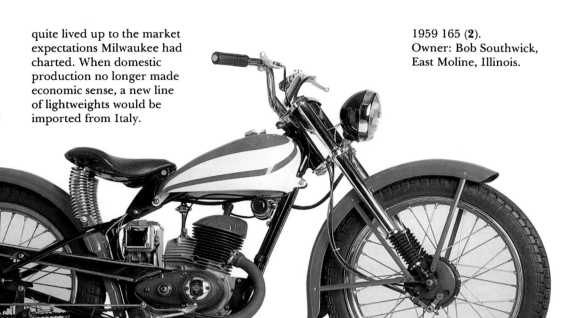

2

the years, including the announcement of our splendid Golden Anniversary models, now in full production, are adequate evidence that we are firmly committed to an aggressive program of steadily moving forward. Harley-Davidson is sharply conscious of our ever-shifting economy, and the need for intelligent and constant change."

By 1954 the spirit of change was in the wind everywhere. Ford built an overhead valve engine, Marilyn Monroe married Joe DiMaggio, and a few hundred thousand North Vietnamese headed south. The New York Giants blanked the Cleveland Indians 4-0 in the World Series, and the Cleveland Browns crushed the Detroit Lions 56-10 for the National Football League title. Bill Haley and the Comets released Joe Turner's "Shake, Rattle and Roll," Elvis Presley cut "Good Rockin' Tonight" and Big Boy Cruddup's "That's All Right Mama." Young America was ready to boogie.

Harley-Davidson somehow managed to maintain a conservative posture in the late Fifties, despite growing evidence of an expanding market for lightweight sport bikes, even Italian ones. The Milwaukee consensus was that the bases were well covered. Sportsters and Duo-Glides were selling well, the Aermacchi 250 was on the horizon, and the collateral police and commercial markets were holding strong.

A number of Harley's eastern European and Asian markets had been closed by political results of the war. The overstock of 750cc WL models remaining had been sold at bargain basement prices. The Panhead received minor improvements and in 1958 the Hydra-Glide became the Duo-Glide with the addition of a swingarm and shock absorbers. The Glide series would spawn a growing family of big twin brethren, 1200 and later 1340cc powerplants

3

The Sportster (**1** and **3**) received bigger valves in 1958, and a corresponding increase in horsepower. An off-road version of the Sporty, the XLCH, was added to the line.

The KR remained the factory racing model. In '57 and '58 Roger Reiman won at Daytona for H-D.

1958 Sportster (**1** and **3**).
Owner: Tom Kowalski, Denver, Colorado.

that became the standard Hog motors. The venerable Panhead was in production until 1964, and the Duo-Glide served for many years as the standard platform for dressers, choppers, cruisers, customs, dragsters, hillclimbers, police bikes and parade escorts.

More of the British imports were capturing the fancy of American sport riders though. The single-cylinder BSA Gold Star was a favorite among those looking for a versatile machine for both road and dirt duty, and racing as well. Matchless and Velocette drew subscribers, as did Norton, Ariel, AJS, Triumph and Vincent. Before long more shops offered German and Italian marques, then lightweight two-stroke dirt bikes from Spain and Czechoslovakia. In 1959 a little 50cc mini-transporter arrived, built by a Japanese firm named Honda.

Little of this activity escaped notice in Milwaukee, but seemed to generate no great concern. Harley-Davidson

was confident in their customer base, unconvinced that any significant number would opt for a British bike and that very few would consider a 50cc tiddler.

A number of their dealers were less certain. They recognized that club level racing – mostly short track and scrambles – was becoming more popular, and that most contestants chose small, two-stroke machines. Very few were Harley Hummers. They also noted more riders going for middleweight bikes, 500 and 650cc twins that offered sufficient power and much better handling than anything Milwaukee had to offer.

The Duo-Glide was little changed for 1959, but for a few graphic touches. The big 74 remained the top seller in the Harley line-up. The large solo saddle would accommodate two adults.

1959 Duo-Glide.
Owner: J.F. Burkhalter,
Bloomfield, Iowa.

The most revolutionary effects on the sport and industry were to come, of course, from Japan. They had begun only a decade earlier, with a clean sheet on the drawing table and extensive files on the products of Italy, Germany, England and the USA. Their approach to motorcycling had no overtones of a dispute between warring clans, no element of a sporting contest between gentlemen craftsman. The Japanese were in the motorcycle design/manufacture/sales *business*, with the purpose to profit its owners and provide a livelihood for its employees.

Little was new in the way of motor-technology since the Twenties. While machines of the mid-Fifties performed well enough, most of the early designs had reached their outer limits. The Japanese decided to build efficient, light and middleweight machines with power, good brakes and dependable electrics. And did. Cams were overhead, starters electric and maintenance low. And they arrived in America just as great numbers of young men had decided to buy a motorcycle.

1

Knucklehead, Panhead, Shovelhead, hike! Three decades of Harley-Davidson development show the evolution of the American Machine. The 1938 EL (**2**) exhibits the classic simplicity of its age; the '49 Panhead (**1** and **3**) marks the stylist's touch of more decoration, plus newer technology and greater mass; the '59 FL (**4**) is little changed in appearance, but the rigid frame has yielded to a swingarm suspension. The clutch/shift units are now hand/foot rather than vice-versa. The FL demonstrates the interchangeable nature of Harley-Davidson components. This machine employs a Shovelhead engine and front disc brake from later models. The slow march of progress was to continue for another twenty-five years, until the revolutionary Evolution of the Eighties.

The Twinging Sixties

**1960
1969**

1964 XLCH Sportster.
Owner: Scott Yates,
Davenport, Iowa.

THE SWINGING SIXTIES

THE HARLEY SPORTSTER was selling well in the early Sixties. The incomparable Carroll Resweber bagged his fourth consecutive national title in 1961, a feat not to be equalled for 27 years. Riders and tuners squeezed more power out of the XR engines, and some of the experience spread to aftermarket products. Between speed parts for the Sportster and big twins, and custom accessories for cruisers and dressers, the business in aftermarket Harley parts grew enormously.

In 1962 Harley-Davidson bought a small fiberglass boat company, gaining its own parts facility for motorcycles and the new line of golf carts. Minor cosmetic changes were made to the Duo-Glide, and the Milwaukee line of clothing and accessories continued to expand. In 1963 William G. Davidson, eldest son of then company president William H., joined the company as styling director. The design touches of Willie G., minor modifications at first, began appearing on various models.

The alleged outlaw element had returned to notoriety, again owing more to the tactics of excitable journalists than to serious bloodletting. Naturally there were some bad customers, and the Milwaukee management had little personal use for some of their clientele. But there was no denying the influx of business in parts and motorcycles. Supplying machines for travel, fun in the streets, recreation and lightweight utility – the bases did seem to be covered.

Harley-Davidson was selling more motorcycles each year, but losing market share. Concluding that a steadily shrinking piece of an expanding pie could eventually have a debilitating downside, Milwaukee scouted several avenues to test the market and investigate new product designs. Not all were successful.

The Sixties opened with that regular renewal of optimism, and Milwaukee was on the move. Harley bought a half interest in Aermacchi of Italy, to import a new line of light and middleweight singles. A fiberglass plant and golf cart facility were added as well. And in 1963, Willie G. Davidson was named styling director.

The film *Easy Rider* (**3**), in which Peter Fonda starred.

1962 175cc Scat (**1** and **2**). Owner: Butch Lightweight, Jeromesville, Ohio.

One market research study showed, or purported to show, that the American motorcyclist was generally uninterested in and not going to purchase a four-cylinder motorcycle. And, given the long absence of fours on the American market, the claim seemed appropriate. Eighteen months later the Honda CB750 Four was on the American showroom floor.

Another, more directly costly, endeavor was the development program undertaken with Porsche to build the Nova engine a few years later. Several prototypes of the overhead cam V-four were built, but the engine never went into production. The project became a $10 million drainpipe.

The AMA had grown more independent over the years, though not unscathed by mismanagement and corruption in its own ranks. But the organization at least

2

came to represent a wider framework of riders and manufacturers than it had in the past. They remained unified with Harley-Davidson in deploring the lawless few whose wanton behavior besmirched the entire motorcycle community. But at best it was an obligatory defense against being tarred with an indiscriminate brush. The loud crowd who had been tagged as "one-percenters" and the "filthy few" adopted the labels gladly, wearing them as patches on their denim vests. And despite semi-serious offers from Milwaukee to supply them with Hondas, there was just no way to get those brutes off their Harleys.

California in the mid-Sixties was more strangely plagued than ever, though several eastern and mid-western areas experienced random outbursts of hairy horrors. The motor-cycle gang menace was taken quite seriously by local law enforcement agencies and the news media. Against the flaming backdrop of American social drama at the time, however, the outlaw biker chapter became just another tempest of teapot dimensions.

Of course, the issue never really goes away. An official Harley-Davidson news release of 1992 stated: "The 1950s and 1960s saw the explosion of the American 'motorcycle culture,' with black leather jackets becoming not only a statement of fashion, but of a preferred lifestyle. The tough 'Wild Ones' image, made popular by the Marlon

3

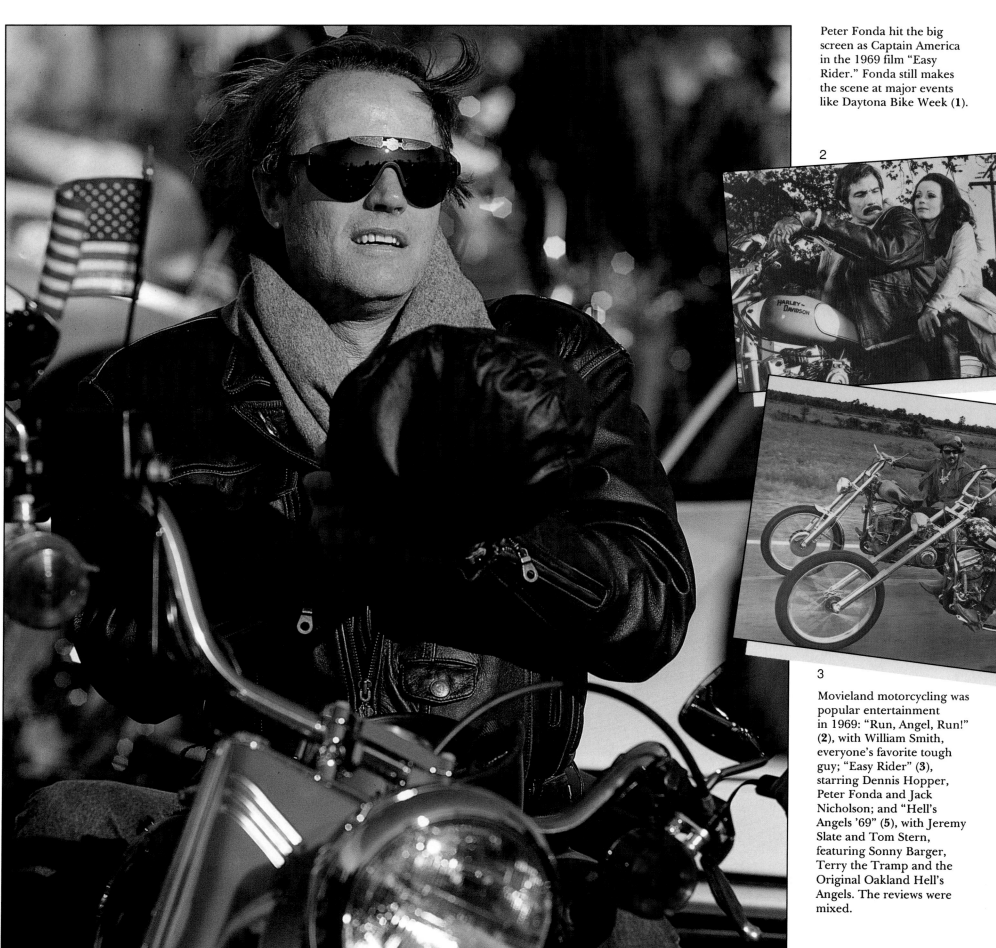

Peter Fonda hit the big screen as Captain America in the 1969 film "Easy Rider." Fonda still makes the scene at major events like Daytona Bike Week (**1**).

2

3

Movieland motorcycling was popular entertainment in 1969: "Run, Angel, Run!" (**2**), with William Smith, everyone's favorite tough guy; "Easy Rider" (**3**), starring Dennis Hopper, Peter Fonda and Jack Nicholson; and "Hell's Angels '69" (**5**), with Jeremy Slate and Tom Stern, featuring Sonny Barger, Terry the Tramp and the Original Oakland Hell's Angels. The reviews were mixed.

1

4

5

Brando movie of the same name, incorrectly labeled those whose lifestyles revolve around their motorcycles as 'outlaws.' While a very small 'outlaw' element – estimated at less than one percent of all motorcyclists – does exist, today's Harley-Davidson rider is most likely to be an educated person from an above-average-income family – in short, the person next door."

That, of course, depends largely on where you might live. But there were times in the Sixties when the irritation level reached the reaction point, especially among racers just trying to make enough money to stay in the game.

In 1965 the AMA held a national 250cc roadrace at Nelson Ledges, Ohio. As usual, a few days prior to the event, rumors began that the Hell's Angels were on their way to it. This advance scuttlebutt, which preceded every major event in those days, made the rounds and the numbers grew as race day approached. Soon the gang was in the hundreds, sure to reach battalion strength upon arriving at the track.

"... like Genghis Khan on an Iron Horse... Frenchy, Little Jesus, the Gimp, Blind Bob, Gut, Buzzard, Zorro, Hambone, Clean Cut, Terry the Tramp, Mouldy Marvin, Mother Miles, Dirty Ed, Chuck the Duck, Fat Freddy, Filthy Phil, Charger Charley the Child Molester, Crazy Cross, Puff, Magoo, Animal and at least a hundred more, tense for the action, long hair in the wind, beards and bandanas flapping..." from "Losers and Outsiders" (4), by Hunter S. Thompson, *The Nation*, May, 1965.

1963 XLCH with flat bars, straight pipes and rigid rear struts.
Owner: Bob Southwick, East Moline, Illinois.

Also as usual, the rumors proved to be wild exaggerations, and the number of rowdies on hand was estimated at maybe fifty, none of whom displayed the grinning winged skull emblem of the Hell's Angels. But most wore the customary costume, rode Harleys and upped the horseplay level as the beer supply dwindled.

The line got crossed during an intermission in the racing program, when some of the celebrants decided it might be even more fun to take their bikes out on the track. Apparently they would show the crowd what a real motorcycle could do.

Texas racer Buddy Elmore was working on his Triumph at trackside when the first entertainer pulled his hog on to

"I got myself some costumes
That scandalize my folks,
The Mountain Man and the Fu Manchu
And the Renegade Cowpoke's,
And when I ride my motorbike
It's to Attila the Hun,
Just another middle class white boy
Out tryin' to have some fun."

from the song *Middle Class White Boy*
Mose Allison.

The Sportster went mostly unchanged in the Sixties. It was rewarded with better breathing in '66, which added a few horsepower, and electric start became an option in '67. The 74-cubic-inch (1200cc) Electra Glide got a new set of aluminum heads, and was known thereafter as the Shovelhead.

the starting grid and began to rev the engine. Elmore looked at the guy for a few seconds, picked up the stool he'd been sitting on, slowly walked over and bashed him off his motorcycle. That was the cue everyone had been waiting for, and as the remaining rowdies approached their fallen comrade, riders and mechanics came from the pits and spectators converged from the other side. A human corridor formed, leading to the exit, and the interlopers were instructed to follow it to the road. Which they did.

Dick Mann went on to win the race that day aboard a two-stroke Yamaha, a portent of things to come. Mann was everybody's favorite privateer, and always had a cheering section urging the underdog against the supremacy of the

The final generation of the Hummer would come in the Sixties. Matured to a full 175cc engine, the line included the street-legal Pacer (**1** and **3**), the dual-purpose Scat and the off-road only Ranger. Hordes of pimply adolescents would descend on school playgrounds and day care centers throughout the land, with unmuffled engines screaming and clouds of acrid blue smoke drifting across the landscape. The children

would scatter in terror as the young hooligans rode roughshod through their ranks. Another strange tale from the Twilight Zone.

Young competitors on a tight budget could press the 175 into service as a production roadracer.

The multi-purpose two-strokes were street bikes, dirt trackers and motocrossers.

'63 Short tracker (**2**). Owner: Kenny Thomas, Murray, Kentucky.

'63 Pacer (**3**). Owner: Jim Allen, Holland, Michigan.

1

2

3

mighty Harley factory team. In 1963 he had edged Harley's Roger Reiman by one point to win the national championship. In the late Sixties the legendary racing battles were most often fierce contests between Mann on the BSA, Gary Nixon's Triumph and the Harley-Davidsons of Bart Markel, Fred Nix and Cal Rayborn. Dedicated railbirds mark this as the second golden age of American motorcycle racing.

MILWAUKEE EXPERIENCED MORE than a little hand-wringing in those days, confronted by the fact that, in terms of public perception, the bad guys all rode Harleys. Certainly not a new problem, but a continuing aggravation

nonetheless since, according to a hugely successful advertising program, the nicest people were riding Hondas. Being forced to the outer fringes of the business while virtuous citizens were attracted to the user-friendly machines from Europe and Japan, that was just a damnable situation to be in. But beyond the long-standing efforts in public relations and dealer education, there seemed little Milwaukee could do.

So Harley-Davidson still moved with apparent caution. Indian had tried a new motorcycle, a vertical twin aimed squarely at what seemed an eager market, and failed. Milwaukee would, as it always had, chart its own trail

1963 Pacer (**1**).
Owner: Stanley Waite,
Wellington, Ohio.

through the uncertain terrain ahead, knowing the geography was apt to change without warning.

And change it did, although few could seriously dispute that the signposts had been up for some time. It seemed that almost everything in America changed during the Sixties except Harley-Davidson motorcycles. But revision was in the wind, and Harley did progress in its own manner. Critics would charge that the efforts were too little too late. Skeptics would wait for the road tests and the faithful Harley rider would just ante up when the old one wore out or he could afford a new one, whichever came first. No difficult choices were involved; Grandpa rode a Harley, Dad rode a Harley and that was that.

The critical corner was turned in 1965. President Lyndon Johnson had decided that his place in history would depend on snuffing the international communist conspiracy in Vietnam, and convinced the U.S. Congress to let him give it a try. Racial tensions in America, despite or because of the passage of a civil rights bill, were on the boil. And that good old rock 'n' roll had been displaced by the strident yowl of Bob Dylan and the pop harmonics of the Beatles. The USA, disunity blaring in the domestic, corporate and federal halls, was bending in the shifting winds of change.

High performance as defined in the USA meant horsepower and torque in a strong and simple unit. Heads-up, one-on-one, straight line, holeshot grunt-and-go acceleration. Whoever gets to that eighth- or quarter-mile marker first is the winner. No ifs, ands, buts or bullshit!

The Sportster had ruled the backroads sprint title for nearly a decade when the upstarts first appeared from Europe, and shortly there-after from Japan. The Japanese took the American preference for slingshot crotch-rockets the most seriously, and built machines to suit. And the first of these Oriental invaders were of the truly noxious two-stroke variety. Zounds!

Backstreet brawler: 1968 XLCH (**4**), drag bars, banana seat, straight pipes and no front brake. Owner: Ben Griffith, Mechanicsville, Iowa.

Harley-Davidson, much like the American auto industry, seemed at first immune to the clamor in the streets. But like many family-owned outfits well into their second generation management, Milwaukee would have to go outside for help. In 1965 Harley-Davidson went public, hoping the sale of stock would bring the means to develop new machines for what had now become a marketplace crowded with options.

Motorcycle shops seemed to be popping up overnight. Some car dealers cleared a corner of the showroom for one or two lines of imported bikes. The enthusiast willing to make the rounds could have a look at the new Royal Enfield, Greeves, Maico, Marusho, Bultaco, Suzuki, Honda, Yamaha, Kawasaki, Montesa, Ossa, BSA, Triumph, Velocette, Vincent, Norton, Jawa, Zundapp, DKW, Husqvarna, BMW, Ducati, Gilera, Benelli, Matchless, Moto-Guzzi, Bridgestone, Laverda or Parilla. Or Harley-Davidson. The market was a gourmet feast for gearheads.

For 1966 Harley-Davidson improved the electrics on the big twin, which featured a redesigned cylinder head and an electric starter. The Electra-Glide replaced the Duo-Glide and the Shovelhead engine supplanted the Panhead. The Sportster was also available with an electric starter, an option scoffed at by the macho sector of traditional tough guys and embraced by the weak of knee and scarred of shin. The thumb-start Sporty became increasingly popular with women riders, whose ranks were still on the rise. The Sportster also got a new carburetor and cams to bump the horsepower, but nothing in the line-up showed any significant advance in design or technology.

Milwaukee, like the rest of the country, was more or less fogbound in confusion and moodiness. The old ways weren't working, and the prospectus of new ways contained some intriguing but expensive ideas, and what some thought were fatal notions. And the sales figures for the competition were staggering, both in terms of Harley's share and the overall numbers. Harley-Davidson showed sales figures of $16 million in 1959, and were up to $30 million for 1965. But Honda, in the same period, had gone from $500,000 to $77 million, and had jumped in 1966 to $106 million. Something had to be done.

On the other hand, sales were still going up, police and utility markets were healthy, and the racing department was showing good results and generating publicity. The 1966 Daytona race was a wake-up call for Milwaukee, when both Cal Rayborn and Roger Reiman retired with engine trouble and Buddy Elmore won the race for Triumph. The following year the Doug Hele Triumphs of Gary Nixon and Buddy Elmore were first and second. This was deemed unacceptable in Milwaukee. One of the few things Walter Davidson hated worse than spending big money on racing was losing races.

One of the most pleasant stretches of American road runs through Boulder Canyon (2), between Sturgis and Deadwood, South Dakota.

The big twins were usually the first choice of early custom builders. The Sportster was regarded in the all-go and no-show category, until a few young stylists chose the lean machine as a suitable subject of artistry in iron.

Steve Brunello's 1964 Sportster (1) is a good example of moderate use of paint and chrome, achieving a unified effect that doesn't overpower the motorcycle's lines with glitz and frippery. Matching the frame and bodywork color complements the engine, and the handlebar fairing, braided brake lines and dual discs give the front end a clean and balanced look.

"I was racing Triumphs against the Harley iron Sportsters, and they were faster. My Triumph was fast, but not as fast. So I wanted an edge. If they were running 55-inch V-twins, I saw nothing wrong with a 61-inch V-twin. So I started racing Vincents and building engines, and along the way I sought out the expertise of older men. My main hero was Rollie Free. And it wasn't the racing exploits that got me, it was what a decent man he was. Clean sportsman; didn't lie, didn't cheat, didn't swear in front of ladies. And he'd fist fight at the drop of a hat. Loved him.

"I'd cracked up and got two broken arms in one day. Rollie came by and said, 'Well, Mike, are you finished?' I said no, I don't think so. He said, 'Well, it's the size of the fight in the dog, Mike, not the size of the dog in the fight.'

"But he used to give me advice, make sure I didn't desecrate the Vincent name too badly. But I did the ultimate bad thing; I sawed a Vincent off and put a Harley transmission behind it. You ought'a heard the howls on that one. In the Sportster transmission you can change any one gear without disturbing the other three. In the Vincent there's only a couple ratios, you've got to pull half the bike apart to put it in, and you're playing with an expensive museum piece. Sportster gears were a dime a dozen, and I wanted to run the same gearing the competition had.

"I don't have much criticism of the Harley Sportster. They had a lot of power, were faster than hell. Engine design was very good, but I didn't like their combustion chamber. I liked the Vincent better for its bigger bore and shorter stroke. But the Harley had one big advantage, because goddam it you could buy parts for it."

Mike Parti *Restoration Motorcyclist.*

One of the most common sights on American streets and highways for years was the FLH Police Special. Fleet contracts for police bikes comprised a significant portion of Harley's business for fifty years. The running battle with Indian for control of state and municipal police business was a history of back room deals, graft and good-ole-boy politics.

1969 FLH Police Special.
Owner: Joe Martin, Sun
Valley, California.

Life in 20th-century America offered up an assortment of motoring experiences. Internal combustion drove the Industrial Revolution, and mechanized warfare perfected the engines of civilization. Among the peaceful fruits of motorized life is the group ride. In a highway squadron of Harleys, the syncopated rhythm releases the locked imagination. The road resonates with the counterpoint of bass drums in rolling harmony, and the tempo echoes the pulses of the heart itself. You are going down the road feeling glad, life is good, and the spirit soars.

The chopper came to symbolize... what? A lifestyle, an attitude, an ego accessory, a work of art, a thumb in the eye of straight society, a rolling death trap, a cop magnet, freedom machine, expression of individuality, a victory of form over function, or a personalized motorcycle? Or all of the above?

ANOTHER SERIES OF events in the mid-Sixties would conspire to throw a monkey wrench into the works. The outlaw motorcycle gang story, in terms of national press coverage, had dwindled away for several years. In 1965 *Saturday Evening Post* ran a story on the San Bernardino, California, chapter of the Hell's Angels, who were paid to pose for the camera. It was during this period that journalist Hunter Thompson was riding with the Angels in northern California and recording his experiences for a book:

"There is surely some powerful lesson in the failure of Harley-Davidson to keep pace with a market they once controlled entirely. It is impossible to conceive of a similar situation in the automobile market. What if Ford, for example, had been the only American manufacturer of autos at the end of World War II. Could they have lost more than 90 percent of the market by 1965? A monopoly

with a strong protective tariff should be in a commanding position even on the Yo-Yo market. How would the Yo-Yo king feel if he were stripped, in less than a decade, of all his customers except Hell's Angels and cops?"

That's a bit of exaggeration from the good Dr. Gonzo, since Harley was actually at a tariff disadvantage against the imports. But Thompson did write the definitive book on the gang, and rode in their thundering processions on a BSA 650. Whether his choice was courageous defiance or a gesture of voluntary subordination is unclear, but the act itself took some measure of courage. The book, *Hell's Angels*, was published in 1967. More recommended reading.

But the summer of '65 marked the crest of the celebrity wave for two-wheeled gangs in general and the Hell's Angels in particular. Some of them realized that big time publicity had its moments of charm, but that it didn't pay

squat. And for those who did maintain some form of more or less conventional employment, the notoriety was no help to job security.

Thompson nailed it down in one paragraph: "So there is more to their stance than a wistful yearning for acceptance in a world they never made. Their real motivation is the instinctive certainty as to what the score really is. They are out of the ballgame and they know it. Unlike the campus rebels, who with a minimum amount of effort will emerge from their struggle with a validated ticket to status, the outlaw motorcyclist views the future with the baleful eye of a man with no upward mobility at all. In a world increasingly geared to specialists, technicians and fantastically complicated machinery, the Hell's Angels are obvious losers and it bugs them. But instead of submitting quietly to their collective fate, they have made it the basis of a full-time social vendetta. They don't expect to win anything, but on the other hand, they have nothing to lose."

Of course if freedom, the rider's byword from the beginning, was just another word for nothing left to lose, the Hell's Angels came to know how expensive that liberty can be. When the only payback from publicity was likely in the form of a lost job, eviction by a spooked landlord and the right to be escorted through small towns by the local police, it hardly pays for new tires. Thus began an enduring bitterness among the Angels; they might have little reason to expect any reward for their contribution to society, or even for their chosen image as freedom fighters. But they got next to nothing for their entertainment value, while the various purveyors of the story seemed to profit handsomely.

That's why Hunter Thompson eventually came to get stomped, when a few of the brotherhood realized they wouldn't see any money from his book. Thompson probably didn't get rich of course, considering his expensive habits, but his book remains an exceptional piece of journalism that's not likely to fade. The Hell's Angels became a far different organization in the following years. But they still ride Harleys.

And while Harley-Davidson was understandably concerned with this revived erosion of their image, there was still little they could do. It was almost like having a crazed uncle locked up in the basement: you're obliged to feed him, but you surely don't want him in the living room when guests are over.

THE AMA APPROVED 750cc overhead valve engines for dirt track racing in 1967, but not for roadracing. The Daytona roster for 1968 included Rod Gould, Peter Williams and world champion Phil Read from England, plus the rapid Canadians Yvon DuHamel and Mike Duff. Dick O'Brien's team had worked through the winter and arrived at Daytona in force, equipped with the strongest assembly of bikes and

riders in years. Though still a 750cc side-valve V-twin, the '68 KRTT had development help from tuners C.R. Axtell and Jerry Branch. Roger Reiman was on pole with a speed of 149 mph.

But it was Cal Rayborn, the master pavement ace of American racing, who won Daytona that year. He lapped the field, ran the first over-100 mph race average and dropped the previous year's time by three minutes. It was a stunning performance, a display of both Milwaukee's hard-nosed determination and Rayborn's exquisite riding abilities. Note was taken, however, that the 350cc Yamaha two-strokes of Yvon DuHamel and Art Baumann had finished second and third.

ARIZONA ROUNDUP

Rites Held For Leader Of Cyclists

TUCSON (AP) — The "warlord" of a Phoenix-based motorcycle club has been buried here, five days after being gunned down as he worked in his motorcycle shop.

The funeral for Robert A. Little was attended by about 30 members of the Dirty Dozen Motorcycle Club and club members, wearing their "colors" or club jackets, served as pallbearers.

Little was killed Friday by seven shots, fired at close range. Tucson police are looking for several people who they believe were riding in a late-model, light-colored car that served as a getaway car.

No arrests have been made.
Police have theorized the killing may be part of a feud between the Dirty Dozen and another motorcycle club.

Meanwhile, last night, police arrested three Dirty Dozen members at a midtown bar after a disturbance. Officers said the disturbance occurred during continuation of a wake for Little.

Officers said one policeman suffered a cut lip after three men started fighting with him and other patrolmen who arrived at the request of the manager at the Cabaret Lounge.

Arrested for investigation of aggravated assault were John Schilling of Tucson, Julian Grant of Phoenix and John Boromier of Eagleton, Mo.

The '68 national championship went again to Triumph's Gary Nixon, the tenacious scrapper from Maryland. Nixon had mechanical trouble at Daytona, but nobody could have run with Rayborn that day. And the world roadracing community realized that American riders would henceforth be taken seriously as international competitors. Ten years later American Kenny Roberts would demonstrate just how seriously.

Harley-Davidson was working still to maintain the support of its traditional customer base. The number of dealerships had fallen from more than 1000 to 600, but more dealers had increased their activity in local promotion of rides, field meets, poker runs and tours. Amateur racing was booming, especially the newly adopted form of European

The motorcycle sport was transformed in the Sixties. Imports crowded the market, sales were booming and Harley-Davidson was in trouble. In order to upgrade the motorcycles and produce enough to meet demand, Milwaukee merged with American Machine and Foundry, a recreational conglomerate. At first the partnership was not well received by either the employees or the customers. Then it got worse. Harley-Davidson would face its most severe period of struggle in the Seventies.

motocross, for which Harley had no competitive machine. The Aermacchi Sprint had performed well enough for short track, but never became widely popular on the open market.

The last great Sprint race was the national at the Santa Fe short track near Chicago in 1970. Harley-Davidson factory rider Bart Markel was having a bad year and a bad night. Local rider Duane Anderson was in the stands that night, and remembers the scene 22 years later. "Markel was having a terrible time. He barely managed to make the main event, and got the last transfer spot in a last-chance qualifier. They interviewed him before the

race and asked what he was going to do. He said, 'Well, I guess I'll just hang back and see what happens at first. Then just pass 'em one by one.'"

On the start Markel pulled a huge wheelie and the rest of the field was gone. His front wheel slammed down and the handlebars dropped, leaving Markel almost in a roadracing posture. Then he took off, caught up with the pack and started passing people, one by one. "It was amazing," recalls Anderson. "He just started passing people everywhere. It was the best race I ever saw." The win was Markel's 27th national victory, tying him with Joe Leonard's record.

Seats became the item most often replaced by after-market products. The cowboy saddle was popular.

Fishtail mufflers returned as original equipment in the Sixties.

1968 Electra Glide.
Owner: Jerry Christensen,
Bay City, Michigan.

Harley's final great roadracing performance came again at Daytona in 1969, again with Cal Rayborn in the saddle. The two-stroke Yamahas and Suzukis had returned with more horsepower, and the first seven bikes in qualifying were two-strokes. But, despite a power disadvantage, Rayborn won the 200, again lapping the field and finishing with a speed only .41 mph off the previous year's pace and less than one second slower.

An all-round racer, Rayborn also set a new land speed record of 265 mph in a Harley-powered streamliner built by Denis Manning. He was America's premier roadracing star, a fact established at the Anglo-American match races in England in 1972, when he won three events and was second in three more on a dated XR750. Cal Rayborn was one of the most well-liked riders on the circuit. He died in a racetrack accident in New Zealand in 1973.

Harley-Davidson, now outstripped by the faster two-stroke machines, retired from professional roadracing.

THE LATEST YEARS

CYCLES OF DOOM AND EUPHORIA

OPTIMISM WAS IN short supply as America entered the Seventies, and the national attitude was grim. Some half-million U.S. soldiers were in Vietnam, Senator Robert Kennedy and Reverend Martin Luther King had been assassinated, and Richard Nixon had been elected president. Harley-Davidson, despite slowly but steadily regaining sales through the decade, was sold to a bowling ball company.

Milwaukee hadn't necessarily been lazy or shortsighted in the 1960s. Several new projects had been undertaken but discarded. An overhead cam, inline four-cylinder engine had been designed, and a mock-up built in Italy. That was the one market research said Americans wouldn't buy. A 750cc OHC V-twin was also under consideration, and a mock-up was fitted to a modified Sportster frame with disc brakes. Designed to counter the threat of British Superbike racers, the project was abandoned when the British effort folded.

Gene Romero won the national title for Triumph in 1970, and Dick Mann was on top the following year with BSA. After that the British industry slid to history, and Harley's main competition on the dirt would come from Yamaha and Kenny Roberts.

Perhaps the best epitaph for the Sixties was provided by a San Francisco newspaper columnist, who compared the Hell's Angels to the Texas Rangers.

The Seventies became Harley-Davidson's worst decade. The addition of the American Machine and Foundry logo on the gas tanks was not well received among the faithful, and disputes soon arose between Harley managers and

The Harley-Davidson coalition with AMF may not have produced an entirely beneficial result, but it did generate more motorcycles. This meant more business for parts and accessory makers, and more raw material for the customizer's art. The Shovelhead years may have been grim in Milwaukee, but creativity flourished in backyards and garages. And H-D would come to take more cues from the individual craftsmen.

corporate officers of the parent company. Although the motorcycles were still selling and production was able to meet demand, the seeds of discontent began to grow early on.

Although the great motorcycle sales boom of the mid-Sixties had begun to subside, sales were still up. Honda's success in the American market had registered with Kawasaki, Yamaha and Suzuki, who quickly geared up to produce larger, four-stroke engines. The Germans and Italians both made improved machines targeted at specific market groups in the American spectrum. Harley-Davidson, down to five percent of a market they had once owned, was determined to catch up. The question was how.

The answers were at first elusive. Milwaukee faced a double dilemma. Already saddled with what many

In the film Easy Rider, *this exchange occurs between George (Jack Nicholson) the country lawyer and Billy (Dennis Hopper) the biker/dope dealer:*

George: *This used to be a hell of a country. I don't understand what's gone wrong with it.*

Billy: *Man, everybody got chicken, that's what happened. Hey, we can't even get into a second-rate hotel – I mean second-rate motel, you dig? They think we're gonna cut their throat or something, man. They're scared man.*

George: *Oh, they're not scared of you. They're scared of what you represent to 'em.*

Billy: *Hey man, all we represent to them, man, is somebody who needs a haircut.*

George: *Oh no. What you represent to them is freedom.*

Billy: *What the hell's wrong with freedom. That's what it's all about.*

George: *Oh yeah, that's right, that's what it's about all right. But talkin' about it and bein' it, that's two different things. I mean it's real hard to be free when you are bought and sold in the marketplace. 'Course don't ever tell anybody they're not free, 'cause they gonna get real busy killin' and maimin' to prove to you that they are. Oh yeah, they gonna talk to you and talk to you and talk to you about individual freedom. But they see a free individual, it's gonna scare 'em.*

Billy: *Well, it don't make 'em runnin' scared.*

George: *No. It makes 'em dangerous.*

Easy Rider
by Terry Southern,
Dennis Hopper, Peter Fonda.

considered an archaic, outmoded machine, the traditional customer was now alienated by what appeared to be a faceless bureaucracy of corporate raiders, with no understanding of what Harley-Davidson was all about. It was almost as if a piece of Americana had been confiscated. Harley-Davidson, after all, was more than just a business; the Milwaukee plant was something closer to a national monument, a keystone of democracy itself. The owners and workers were not simply components of the free enterprise system, but trusted custodians of an American treasure. Now the sacred edifice was being sacked by an evil coalition of bankers, bean counters and conglomerate suits and ties. Maybe even by communists.

Despite the roster of challenges facing Harley-Davidson in the Seventies, some of the creative explosions of the Sixties produced effects that would serve Milwaukee well.

The first sign of changing designs at Harley came in 1970, when the Sportster appeared with a fiberglass seat/tail section in the European café racer mode. The style was rejected by the Sportster crowd, but the following year appeared on the first factory custom, the FX Super Glide. The first in a long succession of Milwaukee hybrids, the FX was a 74-cubic-inch (1200cc) FL with a Sportster front end.

The Super Glide featured Euro-style pipes and a patriotic red, white and blue paint scheme. It would be known, in a loose sense, as the first factory chopper.

1971 FX Super Glide.
Owner: Tom Kowalski,
Denver, Colorado

The artistic output, especially in performing arts like theater, dance and motorcycle racing, had been quite extraordinary. And in the form incorporating all others, the motion picture, a panorama of motorcycle imagery had come to the screen.

In what almost seemed a coordinated promotional plan, within a few years the films *Easy rider, On Any*

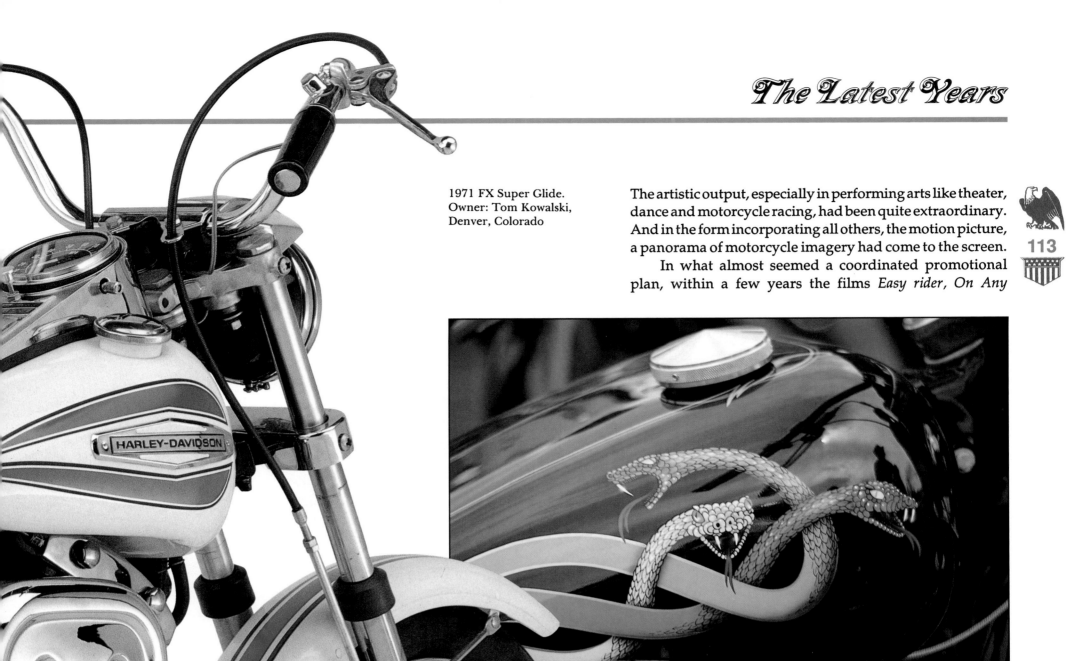

Sunday, Little Fauss and Big Halsey, Hell's Angels '69 and *Electra-Glide in Blue* were released to the neighborhood theaters. Or the drive-ins in some locales. None were big budget productions, but taken together the films covered nearly the entire spectrum of contemporary American motorcycling. Not necessarily well, or with unerring accuracy, but the machines were up there on the silver screen. Larger than life, as they say, and looking, given your personal preference, like a mighty good time.

On Any Sunday did more for motorcycle sport/racing than any film before or since. Directed by Bruce Brown, the movie featured Mert Lawwill, Cal Rayborn, Dick Mann, Malcolm Smith and Steve McQueen in supporting roles. It was a finely crafted testament to the fun and fellowship of the sport, and Harley-Davidson was a featured player. While it may be a stretch to call *Easy Rider* a motorcycle film, it had some good rolling-down-the-road footage and music, and a captivating performance by a young actor named Jack Nicholson. And it served as a life-extension drug for the chopper market.

It's impossible to determine what impact the film may have had on the cocaine business (though considering the Seventies it can't have hurt), or how many Mardi Gras acid trips it may have engendered, but it did certify for a new generation the status of the chopped Hog as a piece of American folk art. It wasn't long before surfers and college students were astride choppers. Small specialty builders, what some call "chop shops" were opening everywhere, and the Speed & Custom industry was reborn. And Harley-Davidson, with absolutely no expenditure from Milwaukee, was the featured player.

The movies did wonders to reestablish Harley's presence just at the time many in the company were having real doubts about its continued viability. They served as graphic reminders that Harley-Davidson was, in fact, still around, and assured the continued attention of many enthusiasts. Hang in there, they were saying. This AMF business may be a bad deal, but we surely don't want to lose the last American motorcycle company. Keep the faith.

By the late-Seventies more than a few true believers had had their faith sorely tested. With problems imposed by manufacturing and assembly plants 300 miles apart, a dissatisfied labor force, and declining quality as production increased, even the most patient fans were having doubts.

1975 Shovel.
Owner: Bill Baltz, Boulder, Colorado.

One advantage of an engine that changes little over the years is the ease with which parts can be mixed and matched. Old and new co-exist according to the rider's taste. This '75 Shovel carries twin disc brakes, aluminum disc rear wheel and molded frame tubes. The historical configuration is represented by the foot clutch and hand shift. H-D torque motors require little shifting.

The spirit of the Old West is a favorite motif among some riders. The painting by David Mann is one of the most popular.

The number of company dealerships was in decline, and the Harley-Davidson trademark was routinely used by accessory outfits having no connection with the factory. The Motor Company was a family business no more.

By then it had become apparent that the company's fate was up for grabs. AMF saw its money going down a hole, the overall market was in decline and interested buyers were being actively sought. Such diverse names as John Deere and Honda were mentioned.

Naturally, some of the corporate debris trickled down to the market, damaging mostly the dealers. Some quit, others added new product lines in defiance of threats to pull their franchise, and some just dug in their heels to tough it out. Some were forced to repair lawn mowers, or even sell real estate.

The outlook was grim. Quality control had deteriorated so far that new machines, fresh out of the crate, might need a dozen repairs before they were ready to roll. Often with no reimbursement for the dealer's labor. Rumors of worker sabotage at the factory weren't uncommon. Jaws were getting tight all around.

DURING THE SLOW, corporate nosedive, Willie G. Davidson was busy sketching new designs and shepherding them through the chain of command. He had taken to making the rounds of swap meets, barbecues, poker runs and rallies. There were still plenty of Harley fans out there, and it was good to see what they had to say, talk about motorcycles and maybe tweak the creative impulse a bit.

One thing he noticed at some gatherings was the complete absence of stock Harleys. According to one story, at one rally Willie was just schmoozing and checking out the bikes when a youngster asked him what kind of motorcycle he rode. Willie told him and the kid said yeah, Harleys are cool. Then the lad asked if his bike resembled any of the customs in the show, and Willie had to admit that it didn't. But, since it was his company Willie told the boy, he could make the motorcycles look any way he wanted.

When William G. Davidson came to work at the family business in 1963, he was a clean-cut kid and had been to college, too. As the son of William H., grandson of William A., young Willie was the third generation of Davidsons to play a key role in the company's direction. His position as director of styling would come to figure strongly in the new vitality in Milwaukee, after H-D had survived the troubled years under the AMF banner. Willie G. (1) is pictured here in his role as King of Sturgis, South Dakota.

At that the kid said, so why don't you? And after a few seconds thought, Willie G. said, well okay.

Before long William G. Davidson had long hair, a beard, and the FX Super Glide on the drawing table. The first attempt was not a huge success. Derived from the Electra-Glide engine and frame, with a Sportster front end, fat bob tank and Euro-style tail section, the FX was a less than integrated design. But it filled the gap between the FL and XL series. Whatever popular tag people might apply – factory chopper, street cruiser, boulevard brawler – the Super Glide was the first indication that change was on the way.

The tail section won little acclaim. "It just don't look like a Harley." And shortly thereafter the bike was redesigned, and the trial and error styling program was under way. Although obviously a hybrid model made mostly with off-the-shelf parts, the Super Glide was a big step in getting Milwaukee back in the playoffs. It managed to cover the range of riders after something between a dresser and a Sporty, a chop artist looking at fewer parts to remove, or drag racers out to build a killer quarter-miler or stoplight terror, or both. And once it looked like a Harley, the FX started to sell.

For 1976 both the big and little Glides were available in Liberty Editions, celebrating America's bicentennial. The bikes featured some of the most psychedelic Americana graphics ever applied to a production machine. At 550 pounds the Super Glide was no lightweight, but many more than the rated 66 horses could be had from the 1200cc engine. Street rod builders could choose from a sizeable selection of aftermarket cams, pistons, carburetors and random speed bits. And with cash and careful assembly, those quarter-mile times could be coaxed down from the 15 to the 11-second range.

The erstwhile Shovelhead still presented niggling mechanical woes, but the hard core enthusiast would make them work. Just take the engine apart, build it the way you want, take the AMF logo off the tank, and everything's cool.

Even though Harley-Davidson was facing serious strife on several levels, the promotional efforts were reinforced and polished up for Daytona '76. The company booked the grand ballroom at the Hilton hotel to display the best of their past and present. The Sportster-powered Manning/Rayborn streamliner was on display, and Joe Smith's fearsome double-Shovelhead 180mph dragbike. Lou Gerencer's XR750 hillclimber was there, a current factory dirt tracker and the Aermacchi RR250, the water-cooled two-stroke twin ridden by three-time world champion Walter Villa.

Harley insisted that the public know Milwaukee was still a potent force in motorcycle competition. Though no longer a factor in American roadracing, Harley wasn't about to let anyone forget their other sources of strength. The sensational Mark Brelsford had regained the national

1

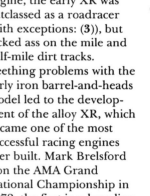

The XR 750 (**2**) was *the* dirt track machine of the decade. Based on the Sportster engine, the early XR was outclassed as a roadracer (with exceptions: (**3**)), but kicked ass on the mile and half-mile dirt tracks. Teething problems with the early iron barrel-and-heads model led to the development of the alloy XR, which became one of the most successful racing engines ever built. Mark Brelsford won the AMA Grand National Championship in 1972, the first in a long line of titles for the XR. The bike was developed by racing chief Dick O'Brien.

Don Emde owns the distinction of being part of the only father/son team to win the Daytona 200. His father, Floyd Emde won the 1948 race on an Indian, and Don was the 1972 winner with a Mel Dinesen Yamaha.

"My first roadrace bike was a Harley Sprint, I think it was in 1963. And I had one of the first XRs, other than the factory bikes. I did come close to signing to ride with the Harley factory. After the '71 season, Cal Rayborn was talking to Suzuki about signing with them. Had he done that I would have been on the team for '72, but as it turned out Cal stayed with Harley one more year.

"So I had to put together my own deal, ended up riding the Yamaha for Mel at Daytona and winning the race. So it worked out all right, but I still consider that an honor being that close to consideration for a factory ride.

"When we went to the Anglo-American match races in '72, I was riding a Seeley Norton for a London dealer named Gus Kuhn, and Cal was on the Harley XR. Dick Mann and I had been there the year before, so I knew the tracks. And Ray Pickrell, John Cooper and Paul Smart had been racing those tracks for years, and they knew all the turns and where the ripples were. It was tough to try to get in line with those guys. I had one year, but for Cal to do what he did was really quite an achievement. He had maybe ten laps of practice at each track, and those Triumphs and BSAs were the fast, high-compression engines, and those guys knew how to ride them.

"Cal would have won the whole series, but in the last heat something in the motor went sour and Pickrell just edged him out. But Cal really shined in those races."

Don Emde
author of *The Daytona 200,
The History of America's Premier Motorcycle Race.*

title for Harley-Davidson in 1972, which was followed by the Kenny Roberts/Yamaha blitzkrieg in '73 and '74. Gary Scott returned the Number One plate to Milwaukee in 1975. The third place finisher that year, behind Roberts, was Harley's rookie sensation Jay Springsteen, who would dominate the dirt tracks for the next three years.

Drag racing experienced a steady growth spurt in the Seventies, and despite the pavement-dissolving power of

Foremost among the hungry youngsters were Kenny Roberts on Yamaha and Gary Scott for Harley-Davidson. The racing was close, intense and exciting.

Kawasaki's 900cc four, Harley engines remained prominent. Multiple engine slingshots were popular with the more serious addicts of velocity and adrenaline. Two of the foremost in 1976 were T.C. Christenson's twin Norton Commando ("Hogslayer") and the double-engine Harley of Marion Owens. At the International Dragbike Association nationals in Memphis, Tennessee, the two twos went head to head for top honors in Pro Dragster. Christenson took

The year 1972 launched a new era in dirt track racing, a time when a few young upstarts would set new standards for speed and fearlessness. The veterans – Dick Mann, Gary Nixon, Mert Lawwill and Gene Romero were challenged by a new batch of broadsliders.

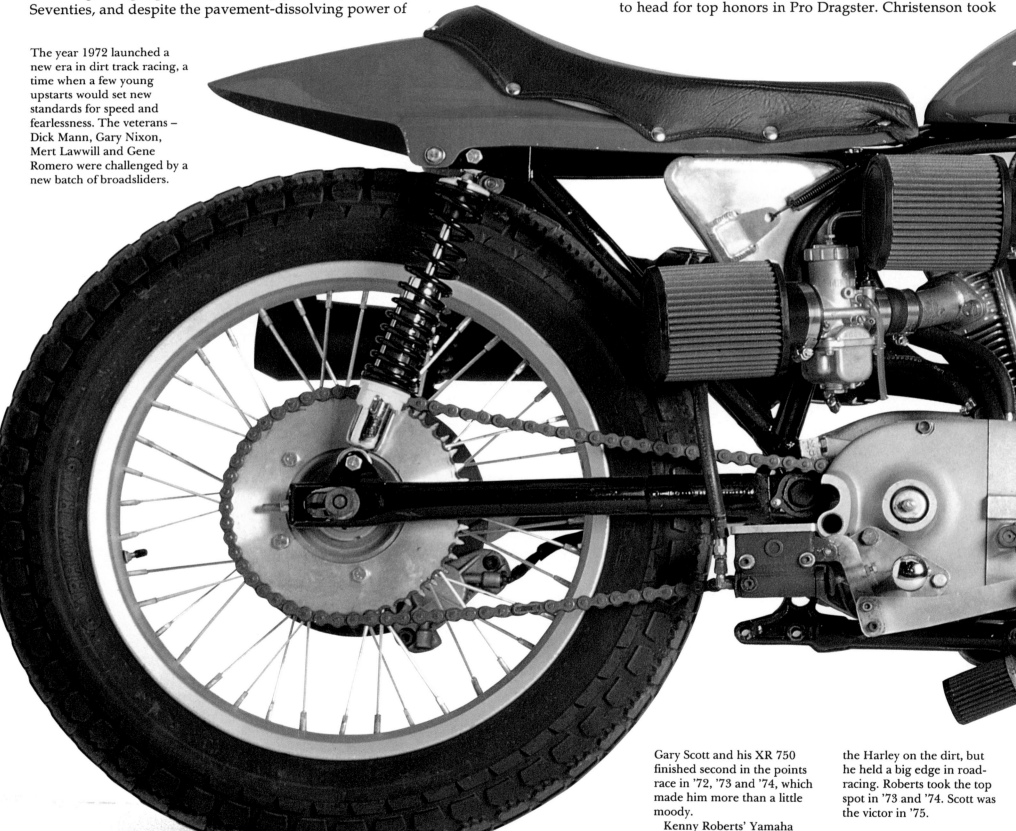

Gary Scott and his XR 750 finished second in the points race in '72, '73 and '74, which made him more than a little moody.

Kenny Roberts' Yamaha was less dependable than

the Harley on the dirt, but he held a big edge in road-racing. Roberts took the top spot in '73 and '74. Scott was the victor in '75.

1977 XR 750.
Owner: Greg Duray,
Hoffman Estates, Illinois.

the win that day with a 174 mph run at 8.49 seconds, with Owens right on his wheel at 8.51. "Now that," observed one viewer, "was some quick fried bacon."

The other form of fundamental American motorcycle competition in the linear mode is hillclimb, which has remained popular since the earliest days. Easily the simplest sort of contest, requiring only a hill and a clock, the uphill dash was the primary testing ground for the first machines and riders. It served as a horsepower gauge; the bike either made it up the hill or not, and the pilot either could or couldn't hang on. Hillclimbing became the first popular form of down home get-together, for rural folks who might only see their fellow competitors once a year, and city dwellers anxious to get out into the country. And to see Lou Gerencer attack a hill on that stretched out Harley is one of motorsport's most spectacular sights.

Another phenomenal young racer named Jay Springsteen would campaign the XR 750 with great success in the late Seventies and early Eighties. Dirt competition got more interesting in the mid-

Eighties when Honda decided to try their luck on traditional Harley turf. In a fairly short span they managed to unseat the mighty Milwaukee team from the throne.

The emergence of the motorcycle as a mechanized framework for craftsfolk would probably have surprised Bill Harley and Arthur Davidson as an unexpected turn in the ever changing realm of motorcycling. One hopes they would be gratified that their creations had engaged so many diverse talents.

In 1977 Harley-Davidson presented another variation of the Super-Glide with the FXS Low Rider, a broad-shouldered, slim-hipped street fighter. And, in odd counterpoint, another Willie G. exercise appeared in the XLCR Cafe Racer. The Sportster-powered model featured low bars, mini-fairing, solo saddle and considerable ground clearance. But the market for European style sportbikes was a relatively small niche, with plenty of competition. And it surely didn't look like a Harley, leastways not a street model.

The CR was dropped after two years, but the spirit behind such a machine lingered in the design department, and in 1984 the XR1000 came out. And it did look like a Harley. With traditional Sportster looks and a big-bore version of the XR750, this was about the most brutal street racer ever to escape Milwaukee. But it was a temperamental beast, demanding high levels of both mechanical aptitude and testosterone to make it work. And it was expensive, and soon gone.

Harley-Davidson decided, in 1977, that the Japanese were making too many motorcycles and selling them in America at unfairly low prices. Their suit was taken up by the International Tariff Commission, which held hearings and conducted lengthy deliberations before rendering a decision. The judgement denied Harley any federal protection, based largely on the testimony of Harley-Davidson dealers that the company was making poor quality products and doing nothing to build middleweight machines.

By this time AMF was preparing to divest itself of Harley-Davidson as a corporate division. Vaughan Beals, an MIT engineering graduate, was appointed president with a mandate to make the company profitable or get rid of it. Several companies had expressed interest, among them Bangor Punta, Caterpillar and Fuqua Industries. As one wag commented later, he would have chosen the latter so that when asked what kind of bike he rode, he could say, "Fuqua Harley."

Opinions on Harley's plea for government protection were divided. Even some faithful supporters were irritated that Milwaukee would have the sternum to require them to trade inexpensive, high-quality machines for domestic iron of low quality. Something seemed to be a little wrong with that picture. Others would allow that Harley-Davidson had taken some strong hits in the last few years, from both outside and inside, and that it would surely be a shame to see the last American motorcycle company fold up. Seventy-five years is a long time. Maybe the Japanese should have to pay more. The arguments rattled back and forth.

RACERS AND READERS of every stripe were also fortunate that the renewed interest in competition produced several literate motorcycle magazines in the Seventies. Foremost among them was *Cycle*, which set the standards for straightforward road tests, off-beat features, in-your-face editorials and comprehensive race coverage. The combined talents, journalistic and mechanical, of Gordon Jennings, Cook Neilson, Kevin Cameron and Phil Schilling were unequaled in the enthusiast press. The original team dissolved in the Eighties, but the tradition survived until the magazine passed through several corporate grids and went out of print in 1991. The best single-volume history of American motorcycle sport was Schilling's *The Motorcycle World*, published in 1974. Also recommended reading.

SOMEHOW, NO DOUBT in greatest measure the reign of Dick O'Brien, the Harley factory racing team flourished in the Seventies. The British were out of the game, but there were plenty of XR750s in privateer hands and the factory

"Back in the heyday of the Easter Match Races when we first went over, which I think was 1972, some of the greatest spectator appeal was provided by Calvin Rayborn on the Harley-Davidson. I remember talking to some British fans before the first race, and they were excited about the possibility of seeing someone roadrace with footboards and a hand-shift. That was their perception of the Harley-Davidson.

"Of course that year Rayborn's XR750, in cool weather and on those short circuits, just absolutely blew everybody's doors off. He set a track record at every track. And he was almost not allowed to go, because Harley was concerned that the XR couldn't possibly make a good showing. That engine had not done well on the high-speed American circuits. That was the last gasp for the cast iron XR; they had gotten rid of it and they just didn't think it would do well. And it was marvelous.

"But after they did that it became obvious that Harleys had tremendous crowd appeal in England, and the promoters made a real effort to have a good showing of Harleys and American riders. The next year we were there with Mert Lawwill, and Gary Fisher as the back-up rider. Gary had done almost all his roadracing on Yamaha two-strokes. I don't remember the exact circumstances, whether it was the flu or what, but Mert couldn't ride at Brands Hatch.

"Someone observed that Fisher didn't have any experience on such a motorcycle, and asked him if he thought he could ride an XR. Gary said, 'Sure, I've ridden a single-cylinder Sprint roadracer, and this could only be twice as bad.'"

Ed Youngblood
President,
American Motorcyclist Association.

Minimalism as applied to the chopped hog means the least of everything but engine. The V-twin is the center-piece, all else plays but a supporting role. The hard-tail '79 FL of Carlisle Guinnip is a good example.

combination of rider Jay Springsteen and tuner Bill Werner was a winner. In 1977 the only rider in the top ten not on a Harley was Kenny Roberts, who would shortly excuse himself to go to Europe and become world roadracing champion.

The Harley engines were putting out more than 90 horsepower, as was the tricked up Yamaha 750 ridden by Roberts. A handful of Triumph, BSA and Norton riders filled out the ranks, but the XR750 ruled. Privateer Steve Eklund used one to break the factory winning streak in 1979, then factory pilot Randy Goss returned the title in '80. Mike Kidd, another independent, topped the point standings with a Harley in 1981, the year both Yamaha and Honda showed renewed interest in dirt track racing.

Honda's new vigor was noted with some concern in Milwaukee. Dirt track was the last remaining stronghold

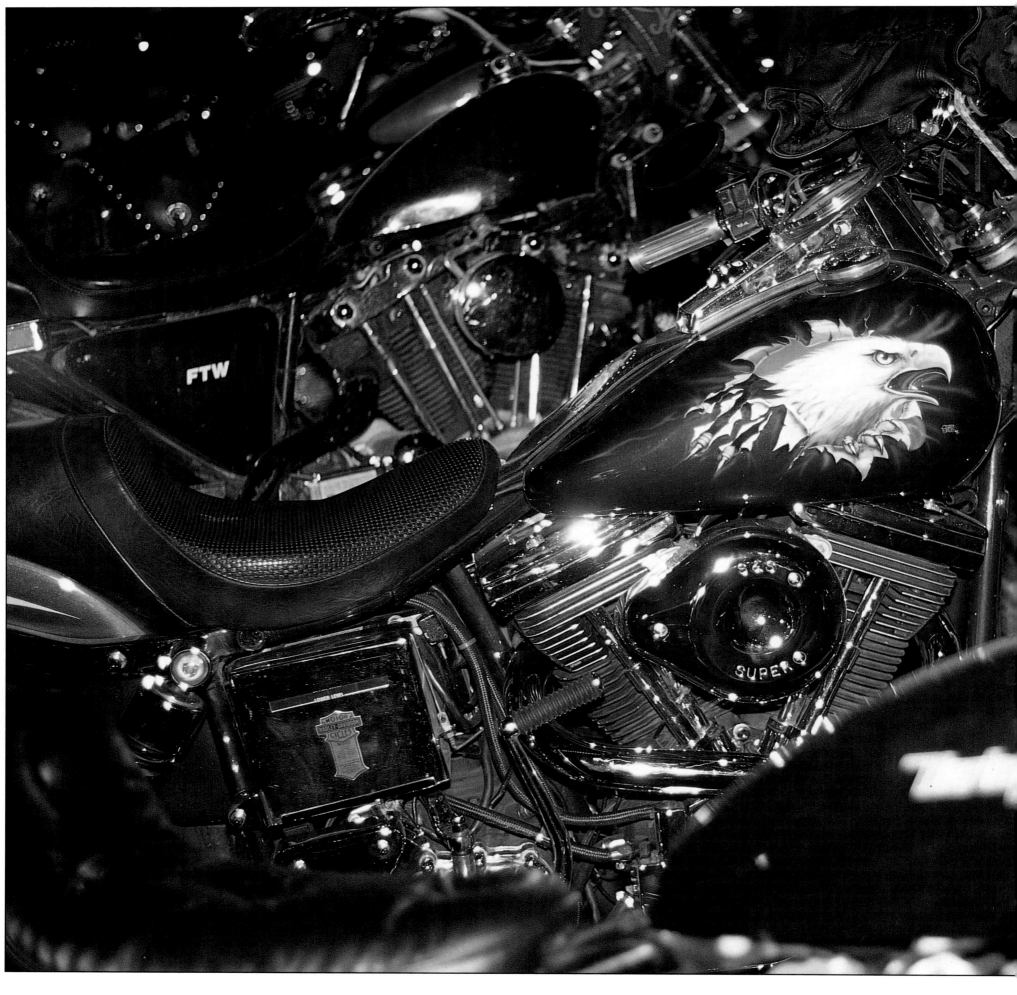

of Harley-Davidson supremacy. Sacred soil was involved here, but with Milwaukee in choppy economic waters there would be no immediate replacement for the XR750. On the other hand, the dirt track crowds were dwindling and the purses followed suit. Perhaps some new players would stoke the fire. Either way, it was looking like the beginning of the end of another era.

By the end of the decade, Harley-Davidson's relationship with AMF had reached the divorce stage, and Milwaukee's credibility with many long-standing dealers and customers had been seriously eroded. They faced problems with the workers' union, a continuing flow of techno-trick machines from Japan, increasingly stringent and expensive sound and emission regulations to meet, and an inventory of aged production methods and equipment. Otherwise the company was sound.

Harley-Davidson did have one thing the competition lacked: the American flag. Following the lead of General Motors, Milwaukee devised and implemented a promotion campaign with patriotism as the basic appeal, and national pride the direct benefit. A block-style number 1, with Old Glory graphics, appeared in the ads :"Motorcycles. By The People. For The People." It wasn't hard to picture old Abe Lincoln himself rolling down Pennsylvania Avenue on a red, white and blue Hog.

125

Patritiotism figures strongly in the H-D company, a sense of pride, freedom and individual responsibility are familiar themes expressed in their advertising. As the sole surviving manufacturer, Milwaukee became the heir to the mantle of Americana. Liberty and Justice are prominent motifs among Harley riders, and some clubs are formed around specific issues to rally members.

Some Vietnam veterans belong to outfits dedicated to the POW/MIA issue. The Rolling Thunder rally began in Washington, D.C., in 1988, its numbers growing yearly. Bikers congregate to urge the government to investigate reports of war prisoners still held in Vietnam and rallies end with a ride to The Wall, which is inscribed with the names of those killed in action.

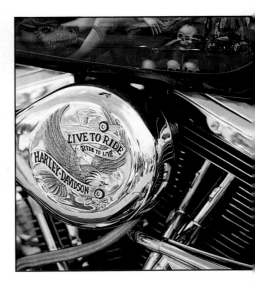

The best place to eyeball just about every make and model of Harley-Davidson ever made: Main Street, Sturgis, South Dakota, in August. History comes to life at the annual Black Hills Classic, and original Knuckleheads thunder out of the past.

And as the Eighties rolled in, with little fanfare at first, but no doubt a sense of renewed optimism, there did seem to be a new spark in Milwaukee. Perhaps there was some kind of harmonic convergence at work, or the spirits of Bill Harley and Walter Davidson transmitted a message from the great beyond, entreating the lads to respect their heritage. Stand tall. Do the job. Whatever the case, the threats of hostile takeovers were thwarted. Vaughan Beals forged a coalition of managers, scraped up the down payment and bought the company from AMF in an $81.5 million leveraged buyout. The year was 1981, and the new president of the United States was a supporting actor from California.

Suddenly the past was on its way back. Not the real past, the one with oil leaks, troublesome clutches, blown gaskets, random carburetion, alarming brakes, snapped brackets and vicious vibration. No, this was the past of nostalgia, the Norman Rockwell renderings of the Forties and Fifties. The good old days of memory.

Remember those days, when Uncle Pete would rumble up on that red 74-inch Harley with a sidecar, surely the finest looking motorcycle you ever saw. And he'd take you fishing, or over to the next county for some apple cider, or on those really special days when they were racing down at the fairgrounds, where men were doing astounding things on motorcycles, sliding fast through the turns, roaring, bouncing, spitting big roostertrails of dirt and appearing to have a hell of a good time?

Or the time Dad came home with that blue flathead and Mom came out on the porch and stood with her hands on her hips, and it looked like trouble until she calmed

Sturgis has it all, from the basic ratbike Shovel to sparkling contemporary Springers, on out to the edge of reality with the Boss Hog, powered by a Chevrolet V-8.

down and it wasn't long before they rode off together, and were gone through four whole innings of the baseball game on the radio, coming home when it was near dark and they were laughing. And dinner was late. Remember?

Yes, those were the good old days Harley-Davidson set out to recreate in the Eighties. The contemporary version would require a motorcycle that looked, sounded and felt like a traditional Hog, but was reliable as a Honda. The first

part was fairly easy, with 80 years of reference material in house. Building a big pushrod V-twin to those performance requirements would be more challenging.

What Harley-Davidson managed to do in the Seventies was much like what the rest of the country had to do, which was to get over the Sixties. Milwaukee was able to buy the time to devise a new plan, do some research and develop a competitive product. Detractors would charge that the

company had to sell its soul in the process, and that they only managed to produce higher quantities of inferior motorcycles. Charges not without foundation. Others argued that Harley was up against the proverbial wall, and whatever they did to survive was what they had to do. And that if it had to be a trial-and-error approach, well, maybe that's not one of the fastest forms of deduction, but the results are usually clear.

By 1982 the design and engineering requirements were in place, and the time had come to determine how best to build the machines. The Harley crew went to the American Honda plant in Marysville, Ohio, to look around. They were surprised. The plant was exceptionally tidy, with a very low parts inventory and smooth running assembly lines. The inspection failure rate was about five percent. At Harley-Davidson it had run as high as 55 percent. The Harley managers quickly realized that their problems had nothing to do with technology and everything to do with management.

Thus it came to pass, in about a year, that the world's oldest living motorcycle company was producing its own modern replicas. And they met with success, in what can only be called a cooperative effort involving owners with desire and conviction, faithful customers, an enthused work force, a few banks and Soichiro Honda.

Harley-Davidson had ridden out its rockiest decade since the Thirties. Production under AMF had expanded, but only at severe costs in terms of dealer and customer confidence. The fence sitters, and some of the riders seduced by the Honda Gold Wing in the Seventies, would have to be won back. The twin reform program, Revolution and

The choice between hard or soft luggage is often one of style versus function. Leather saddlebags reflect the popular cowboy theme.

Evolution, was begun more than five years earlier. Revo – the Porsche Nova engine project – was scrapped. Evo – the updated V-twin – was the star to which Harley hitched its wagon. And they went for a ride.

THE GREATER EIGHTIES

WHAT MILWAUKEE LEARNED in Marysville was much the same lesson that Edwards Deming had taught in Japan

The old-style saddle began to fade away in the Eighties, but remained a common accessory, with or without a fringe.

Front disc brakes became standard in the Seventies. The Electra Glide grew to 80 cubic inches (1340cc) in 1978, the year Milwaukee celebrated its seventy-fifth anniversary. The FLT Tour Glide arrived two years later, with five-speeds and an enclosed drive chain. The FX Sturgis marked the return of belt drive. The FL Heritage Special pictured here appeared in '81, the year Harley-Davidson parted company with AMF.

Two contributions of
American culture
recognized throughout the
world: Harleys and Levis.

The 1940 Knucklehead (1) of Ed Cisneros wears upswept fishtail pipes that were stylish in the Fifties. Some riders extended the pipes above the sissy bar, which on this bike provides a handy mount for handcuffs. Just in case.

35 years before. With their industry and economy in shreds, the Japanese were required to build an operation from scratch, so they faced no history of bad habits that would have to be overcome. In little more than a decade, they were manufacturing the most technically advanced selection of motorcycles in the world. It was a good bet that their methods might be worth considering.

Harley-Davidson did exactly that, and rebuilt itself into a modern organization. The story of how they did it is well covered, from the company perspective, in the book *Well Made in America*, by Peter C. Reid. In condensed form,

the new approach required more involvement by the workers, an efficient production and inventory control system, and a quality control program utilizing the worker's skill to control quality in the building process, rather than having someone else fix it later.

Another assist came in 1982, when Ronald Reagan granted Harley's petition for relief from imported competition, and imposed a 45 percent tariff on Japanese heavyweight motorcycles. But the Japanese simply lowered the displacement of their 700cc bikes to 699 and transferred more heavyweight production to their American plants. So

Vietnam veterans (**2**) play an active role in many clubs and demonstration rides. Militant groups push for fair treatment of veterans and investigations of those still listed as Missing in Action.

131

EASYRIDING

"I was hired on the third issue of Easyriders, in 1971. I'd been back from tours in Vietnam and was going to college and building bikes. I wrote to the publisher and told him about a couple bikes I'd built, and as it turned out he was only five miles away. So he came over to the garage to look at the bikes. And he was impressed, we kind of hit it off and he offered me a job as the manager of ABATE (Alliance of Bikers Aimed Toward Education), the first grassroots motorcycle rights organization.

"ABATE was formed to fight restrictive laws against motorcycle modifications. The government was beginning to attack the motorcycles themselves. They wanted to restrict frame mods, front and extensions and things like that. Helmet laws were sort of an offshoot, so it was natural that the organization shifted to helmet laws.

"We had engineers do tests that proved raked front ends were more stable, that long front ends actually created some cushioning that would absorb a blow before the rider was hurt. By about 1978 we had repealed about 13 helmet laws. Now about half the states have adult helmet laws.

"The helmet law doesn't have a great deal of validity. For some reason people look at it in a very narrow way, so we end up stuck with it. If they try to base any law on the public burden then nothing can stop it. They can outlaw salt, alcohol, anything. It could just go on and on. And the amount of money the helmet law could save is just nominal. Even if you compare it with head injuries in cars, which is something like $6 billion a year. So if saving money is your deal, people in cars should wear helmets.

"I don't think Harley-Davidson's sales have peaked yet. I think it reflects a desire of people to find something they can vent their freedom through. They're selling a lifestyle, not just a motorcycle. Part of it is patriotism, and an ability to be free once in a while.

"Yes, the Evolution engine has had a tremendous amount to do with it. Fortunately for Harley-Davidson they've kept in step with the growing popularity of motorcycles, by putting out a better functioning machine that people can feel will be reliable. Of course I had a Panhead for 12 years; it was built when I was born. It was a fine motorcycle. I kick-started it, but it never broke down on me."

Keith Ball
Editor, *Easyriders*
World's Largest-Selling Motorcycle Magazine.

2

David Weaver's '49 Panhead (**4**) rides on a custom springer front end with a mini-fender. The basic chop: lean, light, long.

3

4

the trade decision was more a symbolic than a tangible victory for Milwaukee, but it did get some attention in Japan. Some observers concluded that the Reagan administration's real motive was to send a message to the Japanese car manufacturers: no dumping allowed.

Whatever the case, by the mid-Eighties Harley-Davidson had customers almost lining up at the door. Movie stars were buying designer Hogs and the California Highway Patrol switched from Kawasakis back to Harleys. Something was obviously going on.

Of course, the best news came in the performance of the Evolution engine, offered in five models for 1984. The 1340cc V-twin was smoother, more powerful, oil tight and it still looked and sounded like a Harley.

Another of Willie's variations on the FX series for '84 was the Low Rider, sporting the Evo engine, spoked wheels, slightly kicked out front end and what appeared to be a rigid frame. But the Fifties fat bob look disguised a swingarm, with suspension components stashed under the seat. The

In 1983 Harley-Davidson released the FXRT, a sport-touring package for the Super Glide. The bike featured air-assist suspension in front and computer-controlled ignition. According to the official company history: "Although the new designs did a lot to improve the motorcycles, the big V-twin shovelhead engine didn't live up to the current levels of consumer expectations for function and durability."

The passenger perch on the average chop is often just enough padding to minimize spinal discomfort.

Dave Anver's version of sport touring is an '83 Shovel (1) in a rigid frame.

1

bad boy look without the buckboard ride. Riders a little short in the inseam were able to plant both feet on the ground, but the solid mounted engine was still a Milwaukee vibrator.

The Sport Glide rendition of the FX featured a conventional frame with air-adjustable suspension, frame-

MAKING A FEDERAL CASE

"That was a great absurdity. Almost as soon as I got to Washington I knew they were dealing with a cold deck. They were engaging in some Jap-bashing, but really weren't concerned about the rights and wrongs of it at all. I believe what happened was that after the buyout from AMF, which was financed by Citicorp, the motorcycle industry took a big dump. So the people at Citicorp – who are bankers, which is the biggest collection of idiots in America, next to the insurance industry – they're saying, 'What's going on here? If you don't turn this thing around, we're going to send in our own people, and you're out.' So Harley-Davidson says, 'Hey, it's not our fault, it's those damn Japanese!'

"Then they moved for this tariff protection, which wasn't protection from foreign competition. It was protection from Citicorp. And they got it, claiming they were going to build water-cooled fours and a whole bunch of stuff. Had they actually done that it would have been a catastrophe for Harley-Davidson."

Gordon Jennings
Witness to the Prostitution.

In 1984 the Shovelhead was supplanted by the Evolution engine, the Blockhead. The re-engineered powerplant was lighter, smoother running and oil tight.

mounted fairing and a rubber-mounted 1340cc engine. The sport tourer also got an enclosed chain, anti-dive system in the fork, saddlebags, and rolled out the door for about $7500. The Evolution engine was turning just 3000 rpm at 65 mph and returning about 50 miles per gallon.

By public and press consensus, Harley-Davidson had turned the corner. Retaining the big V-twin and furnishing it with the biggest engineering upgrade in 50 years, Milwaukee was back in the contest. The Evo engine, which would soon have its own nickname of the Blockhead, was

Harley's lightest, smoothest and most powerful road motor ever. The traditional lineage was preserved in the sound and feel of the big engine, and contemporary performance standards were achieved. The good stuff was there: flat-topped Mahle pistons, shallow combustion chambers, closer tolerances, better breathing, improved oiling and sealing, and smoother shifting gears.

The lads in Milwaukee had apparently pulled the pork out of the fire. What remained was the wait, the long pause before the numbers would reveal how the new

The FXRS (3) appeared in 1984, good news for sport riders who found the Sportster too spartan and the Electra Glide too large.

A DEALER'S OUTLOOK

"In 1983 I was having all kinds of problems putting together the money to start a dealership. I had to mortgage my house, sold my car, sold my motor home. If there were going to be any more Shovelheads, I wasn't going to be a Harley dealer. Then I went to Pennsylvania and saw the Evolution for the first time, got to ride the new Softail and I said, 'Now we're going to do something.'

"I expected Harley to turn it around. There'd been so much grief with the Shovelheads, 20 years of grief. But the Evolution motor has been the main turnaround, and it's going to be the mainstay. Just the dependability of it. That's the problem Harley had; you couldn't go 30,000 miles, or even cross-country, without looking for Harley dealers to put your bike back together.

"Resale value is another main reason people stick with Harley now. There's still a lot of people who could care less what they ride or drive. I've always been involved with General Motors and Harley-Davidson. I've had Japanese dirt bikes and I have a Japanese TV, so I'm not pure by any means. But certain areas I feel have always been ours, automobiles and motorcycles. It's the American thing. They're all learning and buying from us, then they take over our technology and better it, then ship it back and stuff it down our throats.

"I don't like it. I think it's time the major companies in this country get the whipping they deserve, to straighten themselves out and get back to building something nice again. I think the corporations in this country lost sight of reality. What are we doing here? Are we just trying to make money, is that the only important thing? Not the product, the versatility, longevity, the resale value? Build junk so people can buy it faster in order to make more money? It's more than that. It's gotta be.

"Most of the older riders are on Evolutions now. Some of the hard core might have been intimidated by our new building because it looks too nice. Too Niemann-Marcus. I was warned not to make it too fancy, but with a building like this, what can you do? I was against it in the beginning, because I didn't want it to have a 'too good for you' look. I don't feel that way, I don't act that way and I don't want it to be that way. But we still had to work with 20-foot high windows and do some decorating. We couldn't paint everything black and put swastikas on the walls. We had to work with what we got, and we love it."

Bill Bartels
Bartels Harley-Davidson
Marina Del Ray, California.

Most customizers choose a big twin, but the Sportster is by no means exempt.

machines would be received by the faithful and skeptical alike. Meanwhile, the factory was at work on a few new features for upcoming models. Confidence ran high.

For 1985 the neo-classic motif was applied to the FL series, the Heritage Softail complemented by fifties-style fenders. The model least altered was the Sportster, which would gain an 883cc Evolution engine for '86. The Sporty stable would soon grow to four models, including a 1200cc version.

Another take on the Super Glide for 1985 was the FXRS edition of the Low Glide. This sport cruiser had three disc brakes, rubber-mounted Evo engine, increased ground clearance, five-speed transmission and belt drive. Better suited to backroad scratching than its brethren, the Low Glide symbolized a gleam of hope for those eager to see more of Harley's racing experience transfer to the road machines.

Even though the signs were promising in '85, not everyone was firmly convinced of the staying power of the Milwaukee revival. Citicorp, the major loan source for the corporate buy-out, wanted out of the deal. A frantic scramble for financing ensued, with only moderate success. As a result Harley-Davidson went public in 1986 to get its

1

The Evo-motor version of a mid-Eighties musclebike. Arlen Fatland's custom Softail (**2**) sports two-into-one pipe and Dunstall Norton-style front fender.

An '84 FXRT (**1**), a gravel-voiced 1985 FXRS (**3**), and an '85 Tour Glide Classic (**4**) on the bridge to a happy future.

2

3

4

1

deficit under control. The stock sale was hugely successful, and with money to spare which had to be put to work, Harley bought the Holiday Rambler recreational vehicle company. As another builder of "big toys for big boys," as Vaughan Beals put it, RVs were a logical step. Senior riders would eventually graduate to motor homes. Some wondered if Milwaukee would next be looking to acquire a casket company.

THE HARLEY RACING department had produced the last batch of XR750 dirt trackers in 1980. But the parts warehouse was well stocked, and more specialty builders were constructing frames. In 1982 the national title went to Ricky Graham on an independent XR built by Tex Peel. The Honda heavyweight team arrived at mid-season in 1983, with a powerful RS750 V-twin. Randy Goss retained the championship for the Harley factory that year, which became the end of another works racing era for Milwaukee. Honda found more horsepower, hired Ricky Graham and

2

Dirt track racing faced a growing roster of problems in the Eighties. Stadium motocross continued to draw large crowds, but attendance dwindled at the ovals. Sponsorship became increasingly hard to find, and race purses naturally declined. But the racing was as great as ever. The contests between Randy Goss, Bubba Shobert and Ricky Graham were some of the fiercest duels ever seen. The entry of American Honda into the domain owned exclusively by Harley-Davidson gave the racing some variety, and stirred Honda and Harley fans alike to support their favorites. Although Honda departed officially in 1987, team tuner Skip Eaken kept a team going. Milwaukee dominated the late Eighties, as factory pilot Scott Parker (2) strung together four straight titles to equal Carroll Resweber's amazing record.

KING KENNY REFLECTS

The mid-Seventies saw Yamaha join the AMA national championship series, with Californian Kenny Roberts challenging a talented array of factory and privateer Harley riders. The most aggressive racer of the era, Roberts was equally vocal on Milwaukee's continuing influence on the rules governing dirt track racing.

"I have mixed feelings, because Harley was going through some rough times back then. And they were talking about banning overhead cams and things like that. It looked to me like Harley was blocking advancements, rather than doing advancements of their own. When I raced dirt track it looked like Harley was an anchor rather than a boat.

"I tried to get some rules that made sense when I was on the board, and it seemed that everything that went away from Harley's V-twin just didn't work. We were having tire problems back then, because of the speeds we were getting up to, and everything I wanted to do that I felt made sense, they just didn't want to do.

"I know they have improved a lot by getting their own company back; at that time it was AMF. And Dick O'Brien showed such displeasure for it that he quit. I think he was one of the best guys they've had.

"But everything they've done in the past ten years doesn't make sense to me, the AMA or Harley-Davidson. If they wanted a recipe for going backwards, they wrote it a long time ago. And if they can prove that they aren't, I'll be the first to admit it. They're backing up into an amateur show; I think America needs a professional show. We need grassroots racing, that's for sure. But we don't want to back professional racing into the grassroots. I probably made more money dirt racing in '77 than they're making now. That doesn't seem like advancing to me.

"The rule changes that these guys all talk about, and I've never seen it work, are to make racing cheaper. Now, I'm not very smart, but things like gasoline, oil, tires — they don't get cheaper. If you want it to be professional the teams have to make money, riders have to make money, you have to go to the best facilities and put on the best and most awesome show.

"You go to a tractor pull, you're not going to see a John Deere. When you start talking to me about running street bike motors, I'm just not interested."

Kenny Roberts
AMA National Champion '72/'73
500cc World Roadracing Champion '78/'79/'80.

3

Bubba Shobert to put it on the track, and won the national title for three years running.

But the XR750 survived; as a working man's race motor it was much less expensive to build and maintain than the Honda. And with Scott Parker riding and Bill Werner tuning, the antique beast would carry them to four successive national championships and damn near five. In 1992 Parker's Harley factory teammate Chris Carr edged him out for the Number One plate. For 1993, in a move to recharge public interest in dirt track, Milwaukee is promoting a stock 883 Sportster-based class for dirt track to run as support events at the pro nationals.

The Evolution Sportster had already found a racing venue within the growing ranks of sportsman roadracing

At 100 mph side-by-each in the turns, dirt track action (1 and 4) on the mile oval (3) at San Jose, California, stands among the most exciting spectacles in motorsports.

The annual gathering of the clans at Sturgis, South Dakota, provides an American racing panorama: drag racing, half-mile and short track dirt venues, scrambles and hillclimb. A full competition calendar.

Leonard Schaefer adjusts his '49 WR for vintage half-mile action. Hillclimb always draws a good crowd. It's basic stuff: whoever gets all the way up the quickest wins. Easy to watch and understand. Harder to figure is how to fit a Hog motor into an MX chassis.

events. Twin Sports, an all-Harley roadracing series, was devised in the hope of attracting more of the old faithful out to the paved raceways. Although incapable of the velocities achieved in the superbike division, the Sportster class offered close racing, and the performance equivalence imposed by stock rules helps insure that the superior rider prevails. Should the same approach succeed in dirt track, Harley-Davidson hopes to mount a combined series, with a national championship points race on dirt and asphalt.

Elsewhere in the go-fast part of the plant, engineers are at work on Harley's next Big News motor, the VR. Presumably a 1000cc V-twin, the forecast shows overhead cams, fuel injection and liquid cooling, with a race motor in the 140 horsepower range and a civilian model with 100 horses. Speculation on this Ducati-tester has been prolific, but even the most optimistic sources don't foresee a working model before 1994 at the earliest. Keep the faith.

More than several American sport riders consider it entirely fitting and proper that Harley return to the curving paved circuit after its long absence. Having recovered its market for dressers, cruisers, choppers and customs, the next step may well involve a vigorous nod to Milwaukee's roadracing heritage. There's little doubt that the true believers would turn out for a U.S. Superbike series with Harley, BMW, Ducati and Moto Guzzi on the track.

Cards and letters may be directed to P.O. Box 653, Milwaukee, WI 53201.

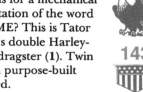

"My favorite Harley story? Well, it's not my favorite, but it's one I won't forget. At Cycle World magazine I was doing a story on a Harley dragbike with nitrous oxide injection. They had cut the top frame tube to make changing the heads easier, so it was bolted together there. When you hit third gear the bike got a severe headshake, so I told them and they said, 'Don't back off the throttle, and the wobble will go away.' So I get a good launch, through second gear, bang it into third and it starts to wobble. I hold it open and stay tucked in, just trying to keep it pointed straight, and it gets worse. Then it gets even worse, goes into a full tank-slapper and just a few yards before the timing lights, it spits me off.

"So I went through the lights at 139 mph, with an elapsed time of 10.52 seconds. But I was not on the bike."

John Ulrich
Editor, *Roadracing World.*

How's this for a mechanical representation of the word AWESOME? This is Tator Gillmore's double Harley-engined dragster (**1**). Twin twins in a purpose-built rocket sled.

All Harley Drag Racing promotes a national series for, yep, Harleys only. They run street, modified and pro classes throughout the country. Current eighth-mile champ is Bill Furr with a 4.63 E.T. The quarter-mile king is Larry Brancaccio at 7.31 seconds.

The FXLR Low Rider Custom was a slick item by 1987, the result of ten years' refinement. The FX series had become the mainstay in Harley's lineup, and was now available in cruiser, custom and sport profiles at around $9000, and the basic FXR at $7000. The FL Heritage Softail Classic replicated a Fifties Hydra-Glide, and the Electra-Glide FLH was offered in a sport model. Harley also rolled out an 1100cc 50th anniversary edition of the Sportster.

Drag racing is the most popular spectator event at Sturgis (**2**). The Minnesota Hell's Angels take the liberal view on components. That's a Honda front wheel.

Another highlight for '87 was the listing of Harley-Davidson stock on the New York Stock Exchange. The company later produced a television commercial featuring a parade of Harley-mounted executives rolling through Manhattan, accompanied by a tumultuous fanfare of confetti and flag waving celebration. The TV spot ended with such a crescendo of chest-swelling pride that one viewer remarked that it made her feel that not owning a Harley-Davidson was almost an act of treason.

Nationalism surely played a role in the Milwaukee renaissance, but engineering had top billing. Harley knew

1

"Harley-Davidson's success illustrates a point that I used to make a lot; which is that there are a lot more riding sports than there are sporting riders. And Harley-Davidson is making a motorcycle for the riding sport, the guy who gets on his Harley and rides down the road. He thinks the little kids see him and say, 'Wow, whatta guy.' And really, if anybody takes any notice at all, they just think there goes another asshole on a motorcycle. Especially when it's one with straight pipes, which some Harley guys seem to fancy.

"I have a cure for all that, and it's just a matter of changing the California law a little bit. If a guy gets caught with straight pipes — motorcycle, car, anything — the officer who nails him sticks the guy's head right down by the pipe, wrings the engine wide open and holds it there until it blows. That's it, no fines, tickets or any of that messy stuff. Leave him with a popped engine and deaf."

Gordon Jennings
Public Hearing Aide.

2

The Evolution engine did not achieve instant success in all quarters. Some of the old guard thought it looked like a "Jap motor." Maybe it just appeared to be too clean. But the functional improvements of the new twin gradually won most of the sceptics over. The FX series won many converts among riders who dismissed the Super Glide of the previous decade. Shown here is an '87 custom (1) and stock '86 FXRS (2).

The Hoosier Hog carries a bank of accessory lighting (3) and a couple of little porkers along for the ride.

3

Of course, The Motor Company also invested heavily in a broad ad program in the enthusiast press, and drafted an outside firm for the public relations campaign to address the old image problem. Even though the Hell's Angels had been out of the headlines for a few years, the old Outlaw Biker tag still clung to Harley like photographers to Madonna. The mission was obvious; convince people that regular folks ride Harleys regularly, without fear of contracting social leprosy or flying into sudden fits of barbaric rage. The celebrity coverage assisted greatly, of course, but not everyone can trust the showbiz crowd. The object was to persuade the blue collar riders that Harleys were now comfortable, reliable machines with the best re-sale value going. And to notify the emerging white collar clientele that a Harley-Davidson was not only the keenest fashion

In 1985 the Heritage Softail (**1**) announced Harley's return to the moto-costume of an earlier era. The new member of the FL family replicated the front end of the '49 Hydra-Glide and the hard-tail frame of the 50s, with suspension components artfully hidden. The old timey look was combined with modern performance, and it was a hit.
Billy Idol (**2**) gets some snarling practice in the saddle of his Springer; Jon Bon Jovi (**3**) reclines on a big twin, and Elizabeth Taylor's Sportster (**4**), a present from Malcolm Forbes, is unmistakeably personalized.

full well that its stake would depend on attracting new riders and a decent number of older enthusiasts who either hadn't ridden for some years or had switched camps. And that those who had migrated to some of the Japanese luxury flagships would require some real friendly persuasion.

Since Harleys obviously look much the same as they always have, and still mix and match elements of styles from the Thirties through Fifties, the essential force for change was the Evolution engine. By 1988, four years after the Evo's intro, Harley-Davidson's production had risen to 38,000 machines. In the next four years it doubled.

So Milwaukee had plenty to celebrate at their 85th anniversary party in 1988. The re-start had been shaky at best, but five years produced some really gratifying results. There had been no batch of motorcycle movies to sweeten the pot, but there seemed no shortage of movie stars showing up in photo features in the entertainment media. Elizabeth Taylor, Mickey Rourke, Arnold Schwarzenegger and Jay Leno offered quite a celebrity spectrum for the public, and it wasn't long before the Designer Harley fad caught on in Beverly Hills. The publicity value of Malcolm Forbes or Reggie Jackson smiling in the saddle was all but incalculable. Harley-Davidson in the Eighties surely became the world's leading recipient of free motorcycle advertising.

1

2

Milwaukee was Hog Heaven
in 1988 for the Harley-
Davidson 85th anniversary
celebration. Some 35,000 of
the faithful were on hand
for the party. If the trend
continues, the centennial
bash in 2003 figures to draw
upwards of 200,000 party
animals.

The design department (**3**) at Harley-Davidson has a relaxed atmosphere, reflecting the character of its director. Here the ideas take shape, are examined, discussed and evaluated long before any production plans are made.

2: 1989 Softail springer.

statement on the motor market, which would graphically distinguish them from the crowd of auto-bound lemmings, but also offer them a taste of life on the wild side. And the justification to wear leather clothing.

Phase Two of the program involved selling the new theme to the more stubborn dealers who clung to the old style. No matter how appealing the motorcycles themselves might be, a junk shop showroom staffed with some greaseballs got up as pirates was not Milwaukee's idea of persuasive sales technique.

The company also knew that a sizeable portion of the new customer group would come from people who had either owned a bike in high school or college, or had wanted to. And that, regardless of social or economic

Willie G. and his wife Nancy (**4**) are regulars at the major gatherings, and are often surrounded by fans seeking autographs.

As a fund-raiser, the anniversary event raised more than a half-million dollars for the Muscular Dystrophy Association.

In 1970 Cal Rayborn piloted a single-engine H-D powered streamliner to a new record of 265 mph at Bonneville. In 1978 Don Vesco set a new motorcycle land speed record of 318 mph in a twin Kawasaki-powered liner. In 1989 the Harley-powered machine sponsored by *Easyriders* magazine established a new record of 322 mph. Some 10,000 of the magazine's readers contributed $25 each to have their names listed on the streamliner. The quarter-million dollars built a 24-foot torpedo with two 74-cubic-inch (1200cc) Harley V-twins built by Keith Ruxton and Micah McClosky. Dave Campos sat at the road rocket's controls. The *Easyriders*/American Bikers Land Speed Record is as yet unbroken.

Vance Breese is chasing the mono-engine record with a 102-inch Sportster liner, 16 feet long and 22 inches high. Achieving that, Breese aims to break the *Easyriders* mark with the same machine.

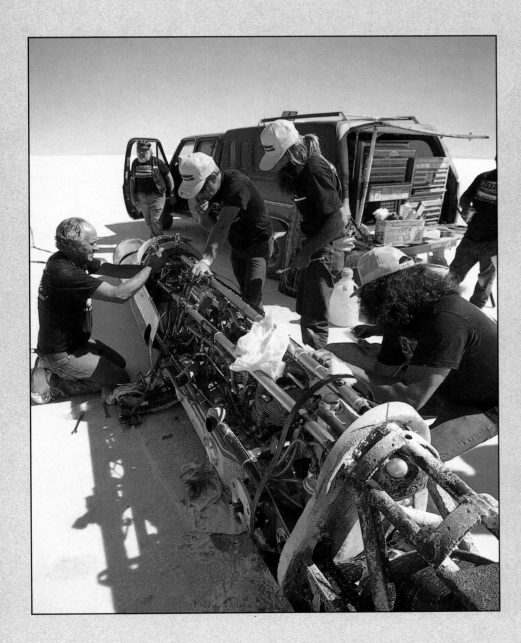

status, most of those prospects had assumed family responsibilities in later years that put motorcycles financially out of reach. But the desire was still there. And the research showed that the brand of choice, especially among potential first-time buyers, was Harley-Davidson. So the logical plan was to make it easier for them to buy a bike.

The first step was to build a better motorcycle, then provide a friendly shopping atmosphere, put an attractive price on the entry-level machines, and even help scout up a group of like-minded enthusiasts for the newcomers to go riding with.

So many a Harley shop was transformed into a clean, well-lighted place, with sober sales people in clean clothes. Included in the price of a new machine came membership in the Harley Owners Group (HOG), with group rides sponsored by the local dealer, regional and national rallies, emergency pick-up service and an international rental program for riders vacationing abroad.

At this writing the combined programs have been in place for ten years. Harley-Davidson's sales have tripled. It was the HOG decade.

Not that the caveman with an attitude has suddenly gone to extinction. He is still there, in small shops and garages throughout the land, cutting, welding, grinding and cursing the yuppie scum who would dare presume to

153

Motorcycling is a family sport, and despite the relatively few sidecars seen on the road, many a youngster still gets an early introduction to the world of two-wheelers. Imagine the challenge of explaining to the boy that the bison parked in front of Sturgis Harley-Davidson is in fact a motorcycle!

Of course when the family reaches a certain size, the time has come for Mom to have her own motorcycle. A far more common sight these days than ever before. That means that Dad's bike has room for the rest of the family, in this case the little guy up front and the dog in the back.

Daytona Beach in March and Sturgis in August have a lot in common. Each has plenty of partying, racing, cruising, drinking, shopping, partying, cruising, officers of the law, outrageous bikes of every conceivable sort, partying, drinking and so forth. An overall mood of good cheer prevails and fights are rare. There are always a number of arrests for minor infractions of the penal code, and charges of police harassment are common and not always unfounded. Large numbers of people on motorcycles still make cops nervous, but most busts are for disorderly conduct (drunk) and citations for equipment violations. The vast majority have a good time, just enjoying the wonderous patchwork of people and machines.

1

co-opt his lifestyle. Of course he will likely accept work from customers of all persuasions because, what the hell, times are tough and at least it's a Harley and not some junk riceburner. In the end, the chronically image-conscious at either end of the biker continuum tend to call a truce on the common ground of Harley addiction, and more bikes on the road means more work for both dealers and independent shops. But they're rarely seen at the same bridge table.

Harley-Davidson does expend considerable effort to persuade customers that authorized dealer service is the best choice, which is often true. A strong dealer who can keep good mechanics will see most of his sales back for service, and the dealer who can't won't. The Evolution engine has sort of worked to equalize the odds, in that it generally runs better longer and requires few major repairs. But the rider victimized by shabby work at the dealership soon learns the name of the best solo wrench in town.

Nevertheless, there's no harm in having allies in both quarters. Socializing and browsing in the boutique stores has its moments, as does hanging out at Sonny's, where there's beer in the refrigerator.

As the Eighties drew to a close, Harley-Davidson had re-established its dominant position in the heavyweight market. The combined effects of an improved product, shrewd advertising and a growing faction of white-collar customers had generated success in a restrained marketplace. In 1989 the Heritage Softail (**1**) was in its fifth year of production, and was joined by the Tour Glide and Electra Glide Ultra Classics. After nearly twenty years, Milwaukee was back in control of the big bike scene.

155

2

THE UPSCALE SWING in the Harley marketing profile is reflected in the growth of their MotorClothes and Accessories divisions. The sales figures for clothing went from $3 million in 1984 to $8 million in 1992. A good looking scooter demands a stylish rider. With $15,000 machines at the top end, what's another grand for an outfit?

The Softail line included five models as the decade turned, including the retro-bike of the era in the Springer.

In terms of appearance, the Sportster (**2**) remained the least changed machine in the line-up. But in 1988 it did appear in a 1200cc version with better suspension. And more change was coming.

Custom builders were keen on the Springer Softail, and ape hanger handlebars came back into fashion. Harley's clothing and accessory lines continued to grow, adding sneakers, underwear, beer, telephones and swimsuits.

The machine rides on a modified replica of the 1948 leading-link, girder-and-springs front fork, with the addition of a hydraulic damper for better wheel control. The Springer came out at $10,500 and was an instant hit, and now carries into its fifth year of production. As Milwaukee grew more adept at multiple variations on a theme, so grew their confidence to experiment with limited production bikes to test the market.

In 1990 the revival extended in the FL series with the introduction of the Fat Boy, another Fifties-style take based on the popular Heritage Softail. With its Wide Glide front end, disc wheels, high/low pipes and flared fenders, the chubby one's monochrome motif enhanced the Buck Rogers' style and set it apart from everything else on the road. And for 1991, as if Harley had to hit the streets with one surprise after another, the Sportster got a five-speed transmission. Backroad riders, who had long bemoaned the lack of sporting character in the Sporty, were all but astounded. And unanimously pleased.

The same model year brought the return of the Sturgis badge, which had been applied a decade earlier to a Willie G. special. The new FXDB Dyna Glide Sturgis had a new, rectangular-section backbone frame and redesigned rubber mounts for the 1340cc twin. With 65 inches of wheelbase and the fork rake at 32 degrees, the newest FX became the

longest, lowest looking dude on the block. Outfitted in basic black and chrome, the Sturgis profile demanded attention without extraneous glitz.

Whatever the overall category might be termed – cruisers, customs, low riders – Harley-Davidson had cornered the market. The pretenders from Japan, a few of which

caught some of the look but little of the substance, had dwindled in the Eighties. Only a few Oriental versions remain, and pose no threat to Harley's market grip. The Honda Shadow, Kawasaki Vulcan and Suzuki Intruder each approach the Yankee style in different fashion, and all sell for considerably less than the Harley. But none can grasp the overall effect, from either the rider's or spectator's point of view.

The Sturgis, a limited-edition model, was gone from the roster in 1992, but the Dyna-Glide chassis transferred to the FXDB Daytona and FXDC Custom models. The Daytona was distinguished by its black engine, gold trimmed wheels and badges designating its celebration of the 50th Daytona Bike Week. Featuring Harley's first "true pearl" paint job, the Daytona also had a limited run of 1700, and sold for $12,000.

Milwaukee's demographic profile for 1991 showed that Harley owners were 95 percent male, had a median age of 38.5 years and a personal income of $40,000. And 62 percent were married.

2

According to Peter C. Reid in *Well Made in America* "Almost 96 percent of Harley buyers are male, and even under the best of economic circumstances they often have to overcome intense spousal resistance before they feel they can make the plunge without serious domestic complications."

ON AUGUST 5, 1991, Soichiro Honda died at the age of 84. He was among the century's handful of moto-visionaries. That vision produced a new era for motorcycling worldwide, and helped pave the way for the revitalization of Harley-Davidson.

As a corollary of Harley-Davidson's success there was a concurrent rise in the speed equipment business. While most riders put their major emphasis on the bike's appearance, a significant number choose to alter the performance first. *Cycle World* magazine examined a 1990 FXR Low Rider set up by S&S Speed Equipment in Wisconsin and an '86 Sportster built by Carl's Speed Shop in California. The object was to compare the performance with their stock counterparts. The FXR, with drag specialist Jay Gleason aboard, bolted to a 10.8-second quarter mile time at a top speed of 126 mph. That's roughly three seconds quicker and 28 mph faster than a stocker. The S&S motor displaced 1868cc and reportedly pumped out 163 horsepower on the

dyno, a power boost that costs about $6000. The Sportster, ridden by young Don Canet, turned a 10.94 at just under 126 mph. On the open road the Sporty topped out at 145 mph.

Given sufficient monetary injections and an experienced hand, Harleys can obviously be made to go very fast. One problem some prospective buyers have faced in recent years is how quickly some models disappear from the showroom floor. A noteworthy statistic on Harley-Davidson's flow chart is the increase in the percentage of its production shipped overseas. That number doubled in five years. In terms of the numbers of motorcycles sold abroad, that works out to about 6000 in 1987 and 20,000 in 1992. This created some hard feelings among dealers who had more orders than motorcycles. The export policy has ostensibly been changed, and the percentage sent out of the country reduced.

In domestic sales, the overall street bike market in the U.S. has been almost flat for five years, except for Harley-Davidson. Some dealers say they could sell 10 to 20 percent more machines than they can get. Others voice concern that too many motorcycles could flood the market and depress sales and resale values. Of course, no one knows whether or not Harley's phenomenal climb will continue at the same rate, flatten out or start to drop. With a production schedule of 77,000 machines for 1993, up nearly 10 percent

The Nineties found H-D in a comfortable position. Still selling all the machines they could build, the company was able to experiment further with limited run specials and to try out some new custom touches in the marketplace. The time was now right, the time Willie G. had been working toward for the past thirty years. The New Good Old Days. The FL line got a new Fat Boy (1), with disc wheels, staggered pipes and pigskin seat. The all silver '90 edition evoked science fiction images of the Forties. The Tour Glide Ultra Classic (2) got four-speaker stereo and CB radio. The Sturgis was back, reframed with rubber motor mounts.

"I agree with the factory's philosophy of creating demand overseas. If we had more bikes here we would almost flood the market and you'd get back into discounting, and the used bikes would go down in value. This way it creates a better demand if you come up a little short. The growth is the same, in the amount they ship here and abroad.

"But for the dealers, every time you sell a bike overseas you sell your future away. That bike doesn't come back for service, the customer doesn't come back in for clothing or any of the other goodies that Harley offers. Tom Perkins used to sell bikes by the lot overseas, and I would play a little joke on him. When people would come in and want a bike to ship to Europe, I'd give them a note with Tom's name on it and send them to him. I'd say he was the head of overseas sales for Harley-Davidson.

"I'm more pro-factory than some dealers. I look at it like a marriage; I joined up with Harley and I'll go the Harley line however they want to do it. If not, you get a divorce. That's what I say at dealer's meetings. You'll have guys moan about every move the factory makes, but when you file a complaint you have to file a solution too, instead of just bitching about it. I tell 'em hey, if you don't like it, go get a McDonald's franchise or something."

Bob Dron
Dron's Harley-Davidson
Oakland, California.

G. to turn Sturgis into Hog Town, USA, a theme village owned by Harley-Davidson, Inc.

Main Street is the major scene, the sidewalk and roadway alive with a slowly moving stream of bikers in black leather and denim, silver, tattoos, hair-dos and headbands. Between the constant rubbernecking and eyeballing the people and machines, some visitors slide into an almost hypnotic state of Sturgisitis. This is most often cured by a rest in the shade and a cold beer, or a ride over to Spearfish, Deadwood and back, or a southern run to catch the light show at Mount Rushmore, out to the Badlands and Wounded Knee, or up to the Custer Battlefield in Montana.

Riding the high plains on a Harley was recently listed among the top three forms of physical therapy by the prestigious O'Leary Institute of Neuromuscular Kinetics (OINK) and the Federal Bureau of Alcohol, Tobacco and Firearms.

OINK, by the way, recently adopted the credo of the Society of Torque and Recoil, which is: "If it rolls, floats, flies or shoots, runs on gasoline or gunpowder, goes fast or shoots a big bullet and makes a lot of noise, thus producing Torque and Recoil – it's cool."

Back in Sturgis the street is still alive with the sounds of Hogs, and the talk of the evening's entertainment. That night it's Willie Nelson and Waylon Jennings up in the hills at the Bentshoe Ranch, now owned by a California corporation called the Hell's Angels. The Buffalo Chip campground has Commander Cody and his Lost Planet Airmen, followed later in the week by Savoy Brown, Stray Cats and the Edgar Winter Blues Band. Supporting acts include wet T-shirt contests, bungee jumping, dirt drags, motorcycle rodeo and Hondas melted by jet engines. The Buffalo Chip scene, described by *Spin* magazine as "the best party in America," has been the cause of the most concern among the local citizens.

Racing? Sturgis offers half-mile and short track dirt ovals, hillclimb, TT scrambles and a dragstrip. Harley-Davidson factory rider Chris Carr, reigning master of the 600cc class, wins the short track national, and goes on to take the AMA Grand National Championship for 1992. Over at Sturgis Dragway, Bill Furr of South Carolina jams his Harley to a new eighth-mile record at 4.63 seconds. Among the amateur, professional and vintage divisions, motorcycle racing is under way at one venue or another all week.

For the still-entertainment-disadvantaged there's a Medieval Festival with "16th century entertainment," the Seattle Cossacks precision motorcycle drill team, the Big Daddy Rat motorcyle show at city park, Hamster ride-in and custom show, the Motorcycle Museum and Hall of Fame, the Victor McGlaglen Drill Team and the governor's tour. Or maybe just get a tattoo, fall down and go to sleep.

Visitors who try to take it all in at Sturgis eventually take on the glazed visage of the Hog Gone zone. They can be seen clinging to the bar at the Broken Spoke Saloon/ pavilion/repair shop/museum/cafe, where the menu includes Rolaids and Tylenol. They surface in Gunner's Lounge, wearing T-shirts proclaiming "I survived the Shootout at Gunner's Lounge – 1991," or just kicking back on their bikes on Main Street, watching the parade go by.

Almost every store front in Sturgis is transformed into some form of motorcycle-related vendor in August. Real estate agencies, tax offices, barber shops, hardware stores – the town becomes a moto-accessory arcade of leathers, jewelry, T-shirts, poster, tattoos, boots and bangles spilling out at the edges of town.

The motorhead dialogue in town runs day and night, most bikers plenty willing to talk about their machines. Mike Cole of Ohio: "Yeah, it's an '82 Shovelhead and it's .30-over, got a B-grind Andrews cam and a bunch of headwork, seven-angle valve job, S&S top end. Got the Dell'orto two-throat on it, Ness two-into-one pipe. We've got Rev-Tech wheels and Koni shocks; lot of hand made stuff, and it's 5.5 inches lower in front."

A woman on the street surveys the sea of motorcycles. "Look at all that rice! I can't believe there's this much rice. Ten years ago you wouldn't see any Hondas here. It's

The first and foremost of the Harley customizers was Arlen Ness (**2**) of San Leandro, California.

For twenty-five years the work of Arlen Ness has made him the top name in the field of truly specialized Harley customs. The word unique can properly be applied to most of Ness' creations, and in the case of the Big Red One (**1**), outrageous may be the right term. The crankshaft is a Harley item; the rest of the cosmic rocket is from the automotive world or custom fabricated. From the back, the car rim holds a 265/60-16 Pirelli, and connects to the engine via dual drive belts. John Harmon made the cases, cylinders and heads of aluminum, and the engine displaces 2100cc. Each cylinder hooks to a Magnuson supercharger fed by two-throat Dell'Orto carbs. The pistons are from a Chevrolet V-8, and the sound emitted from the straight megaphone pipes will shatter concrete.

1

A Ferrari fan, Ness patterned Red's bodywork on the Testarossa. The aluminum shell was made at Boyd Coddington's hot rod emporium in So. California.

167

There was one guy who went around to the biker bars and offered guys cash for their bikes. Incredible."

Arlen Ness, king head guru of the Harley customizers, rides by on a low, streamlined, full-fendered Flash Gordon rocket bike. One of the Hamsters putts along on a motorized barstool. A woman in a fringed bikini, high heeled black leather boots and a cowboy hat goes by. Between her breasts an eagle tattoo takes flight. Just in from Florida a young blond girl sports a gold nose ring, a long vine of red roses tattooed on one arm, and

In Memory of
Lenny 6/16/90
Wayne 8/25/91

tattooed on the other. A British biker is telling her that someone had left pet snakes in a closed car, and returned to find them dead from the heat. He can't believe it.

The latest product of Arlen's imagination is a streamlined Flash Gordon convertible. The translucent body, which shrouds all of the rear wheel and most of the front, can be quickly detached to expose a lean and low street machine. Simple by Ness standards, the drop-body is a new twist from the creative master of customs.

become a tourist attraction. No wonder the Hell's Angels don't come here any more. I hear all the old bikers are staying in Spearfish."

Carson, of Racine, Wisconsin, speaks of the international market for Harleys. "There was a guy over here from Holland, buying up all the used Harleys he could find. He'd come into a shop and say, 'How much you want for that one, that one,' etc. Then he'd just add up the figures, not even try to bargain with the dealer, and fill out a check on the spot. Then he'd pay storage on 'em until he could have a truck come pick 'em up, and ship 'em all to Europe.

Mary Beauvais (**1**), one of the loveliest and most pleasant flapjack servers in the high plains country.

1

More than a few bleary-eyed bikers stumble into the Road Kill Cafe (**2**) for breakfast, and walk out feeling a little less like they had been scraped up off the road.

3: a well-plumbed engine in another Arlen Ness creation, Double Trouble.

Following cool weather early in the week, the temperatures are rising in Sturgis, into the low 90s with humidity not far behind. The patrol cops take on a wary look, knowing things can turn crazy in the heat.

Outside Gunner's Lounge a shirtless fellow stops to examine the T-shirt display. He weaves slightly from the waist up as his glassy eyes roam over the merchandise. He seems rooted. The friendly proprietor says, "How'ya doing this afternoon? You having a good time?" No response. "How about this weather, huh? All these great motorcycles, beautiful women and a nice piece of shade …. What more could you ask for?" Seconds drift by as the weaver gives the question some thought, then says, "Maybe a beer."

Inside Gunner's there's no hint of air conditioning, but the beer is cold. Texas Ray says this whole controversy over the Buffalo Chip campground began last year when they had a strip contest. "They had a first prize of $10,000, and it turned out the girl who won was only 16 years old. And her picture turned up in motorcycle magazines all over the country. Well, her parents sued the campground owner, the city, the county and anybody else they could think of. Got a bunch of money out of it. Now they can't sell beer out there any more.

"And you know what's gonna happen don't you?" asks Ray, getting a little cranked about it. "No matter how much beer they carry in, they're gonna run out. Then they're gonna get on their bikes and head into town for more. So you're gonna have even more of a problem."

2

A stocky, middle-aged biker and his Native American wife come by. His T-shirt reads – *Don't Worry. Be Hopi*. A shapely girl in an over-filled halter top, cowboy boots and jeans has handcuffs hung on a belt loop. A clean-shaven guy with the look of a high school math teacher seems out of place.

Hardly a T-shirt in town lacks some elaboration on the Harley logo, or some slogan, creed, advice or political platform. Some feminist twists include *Men Are Animals, But Some Make Nice Pets*.

3

MALIBU MOUNTAINS HOG RANCH

Paisano Publications in Agoura, California, publishes Easyriders, In The Wind,, V-Twins, Biker, Tattoo and American Rodder magazines. With combined circulation of more than a half-million issues per month, the Paisano titles represent not only the world's largest Harley-Davidson readership, but the highest selling motorcycle magazine overall.

The Easyriders-sponsored Harley-powered streamliner holds the world land speed record of 322 mph, set at the Bonneville salt flats in 1990. Paisano publisher Joe Teresi also owns the Malibu Mountains Racquet Club, built originally by tennis star Pancho Gonzales. As a recreational club for bikers, the site drew complaints from neighbors, which led Los Angeles County authorities to revoke the club's operating permit.

Despite long operation under a conditional use permit for recreation, the county was persuaded that the property's original agricultural zoning was more appropriate. Teresi responded by changing the name to the Malibu Mountains Hog Ranch, and adding pigs, chickens and turkeys. Plans were announced to convert the swimming pool to a trout pond.

One planning commissioner expressed doubt that the facility could really be a tennis club when the restaurant was called "Le Cafe Bubba."

Teresi's appeal was denied by the county board of supervisors, so he now intends to file a lawsuit. "This is my stand against misuse of the law," says Teresi, "and abuse of authority by the county regulating agencies. Fortunately I'm not in a position where I have to stand still for it."

1

2

Those who come down with Whole Hog hysterics find them easily dispelled by a putt through Boulder Canyon to Deadwood, just a few miles up the road. The old town has been turned into a large gaming casino, but the character of the old west buildings and brick streets have fixed Deadwood in the early 1900s.

Rolling into Deadwood on a Harley for the first time is a certifiable American experience. Coming up by Carrie Nation's Temperance 7 Gaming Hall, then the Wild Bill Bar with mannequin-prostitutes posed in the second storey windows, the wide brick street runs down past the majestic Franklin Hotel. There's the Eagle Bar (Original Site of Saloon No 10) where Wild Bill Hickock was shot, and the Goldberg Grocery – "Site of the capture of the assassin Jack McAll, who shot Wild Bill Hickock August 2, 1876."

The casino employees are dressed in period outfits, and the tableau tends to take on the patina of theme park kitsch, but it hardly overwhelms the powerful landscape of

these hills. Some heavy duty history came down here-abouts. And behind the hum of the slot machines, echoes of old war chants linger in the background. The spirits of Crazy Horse, Annie Oakley and General William Custer are still here in the shadows.

South Dakota adopted its state seal in 1889. Bill Harley was then nine years old. The banner on the seal reads – "Under God the People Rule." In 1890, during an attempted arrest on the reservation, Sitting Bull was shot and killed.

The best fictional account of this place and time, from the cowboy perspective, is a book called *Deadwood*, by Pete Dexter.

BACK IN STURGIS at daybreak, Main Street is already half filled with motorcycles. Early risers are having breakfast at the World Famous Road Kill Cafe, where the menu includes "The Chicken that Almost Crossed the Road," and "Poodles and Noodles." Manager Peggy has to reassure a young child who is crying that it's just a joke, and they don't serve small dogs. The Senior Citizens Center draws a stream of customers for the $3.50 breakfast of sausage, eggs and

pancakes. Senior Mary Beauvis, in a sexy *Harley-Davidson* top, waves her flapjack flapper on high and patrols the long tables with a fresh plate. "Pancakes," she sings, "get 'em while they're hot. Keep you going all day."

Evelyn Klocko from North Dakota has been coming to Sturgis for 25 years, and stakes out the best bench on Main

3

The Buell 1200 (**2**) is one of the less common Harley-powered machines in Sturgis, where even the police bikes (**1**) feature unusual light fixtures.

The Hamsters M.C. is made up of industry folks who bring their latest creations to the Black Hills every year.

The Italian chapter was represented by a completely flamed entry with mondo bags (**3**). Main street (**4**) in Sturgis is four solid blocks of motorcycles, and the side streets are full as well.

4

THE SPORT BUILDERS

Sport riders have traditionally had a narrow selection of aftermarket parts compared to their custom-oriented counterparts. Steve Storz, a former Harley-Davidson factory racing mechanic, began with a small line of dirt track accessories in the early Eighties. As dirt track began to decline, Storz expanded his performance line for road-going Harleys.

Storz Performance of Ventura, California, offers a complete kit that transforms a stock Sportster into a street-legal replica of the Harley XR750 racebike. The kit includes high pipes, seat and tank, rear set footpegs, Ceriani fork and alloy rims. Storz also offers suspension components for the big twins and high performance parts for Harley dirt track and roadrace machines.

But Storz is skeptical about the proposed Sportster-based dirt track program. "It has possibilities," he says, "but it's unclear where the riders are going to come from. If it's the same people who are riding the big bikes, then all you've done is given them one more expense. That's not going to help. And there's hardly any grassroots level to go to any more. There used to be fairground tracks all over the midwest, that for liability reasons don't have races any more. There are just fewer and fewer places to do this, and you're not going to fix that by offering up a new class.

"Roadracing is another matter. Harley is behind that with dollars, and you've got people already roadracing who are doing it. That's a good thing and it creates interest, but I don't know that it can help dirt track in the same way."

Storz is optimistic about Harley's continued overall growth, however, especially in European and other overseas markets. "We'll be offering more parts for the big twins. Our new project bike will be based on the FXR, and that will have some new items."

Erik Buell, another former Harley-Davidson employee, designed his first sportbike around the Harley XR1000 engine in 1985. Using a light chrome-moly chassis, rubber-mounted engine as a stressed frame member, and below-the-engine rear shock, the Buell RR1000 had a production run of 50 machines in 1987-88.

Subsequent generations housed the 1200cc Evolution engine, and were offered in solo and dual seat models. With the five-speed 1200 in 1991, the Buell gained an upside-down fork and six-piston front brake calipers.

The Buell is a hand-built machine with considerable attention to detail. The powder-coated tube chassis weighs only 19 pounds but is exceptionally rigid. The three-point

Uniplanar mounting system absorbs vibration and allows the engine to be used as a stressed member of the frame. And the fiberglass bodywork gets 14 layers of metallic paint applied by hand.

Available in solo and dual seat models at about $15,000, the Harley-powered sportbikes are built by the Buell Motor Company in Mukwonago, Wisconsin.

Goodman Engineering of Worcestershire, England, applies a traditional British sportsman look to the Harley cafe racer theme. The HDS (Harley-Davidson Special) 1200 features the Evo engine in a frame of Reynolds 531 tubing, patterned after the fabled Norton Featherbed design. Goodman makes the frame, swing arm, exhaust system, oil and fuel tanks, seat and side panels. The Marzocchi fork is fitted to Goodman yokes, and carries dual four-piston Brembo calipers. Magnesium wheels are made to Goodman's design. The dry weight is listed at 450 pounds (204 kgs).

Should the machine seem more than vaguely reminiscent of the Velocette Thruxton, that's because Simon Goodman's grandfather Percy was a founder of the Veloce Company. The HDS carries the traditional Velo black-and-gold paint scheme, and Simon admits his fondness for the classic British cafe racer look.

The Anglo-American special employs Metalstik rubber bushings to quell the V-twin's worst vibrations, and Goodman is willing to elevate the Sportster's power output for customers who want more grunt. The chassis kit goes for about $10,000, for those with an Evo 1200 engine already at hand, and about $15,000 for a complete machine.

Another variation on the featherbed Harley is the 883 XLR Victory, built by Lance Weil of Hollywood, California. This is a race replica of the bike Lance campaigned on British circuits in the mid-Sixties.

"I will be building a limited quantity of up to 25 reproductions," says Weil, "each unique in the smallest detail to itself, as only a tool room, hand-built race machine can be." The frame is Reynolds 531 tubing, the alloy tank holds 3.75 gallons of fuel and the bike reportedly weighs only 345 pounds (157 kgs). The price is $33,800, and orders require a 50 percent deposit.

The HDS (**1**) is a Cafe Sportster with a British accent. Built in England by Simon Goodman, the bike features magnesium wheels, Koni shocks, Marzocchi fork and seat of Connolly leather.

1

2 and **3**: two more bikes from the streets of Sturgis. For those considering gold plating for numerous hard parts on their Harley, it may well prove nearly as costly as a Rolex.

Turbocharged Harleys are not common sights on the street. The big V-twin does not lend itself especially well to some high performance modifications. Maybe the hard saddle serves as a reminder to hang on very tightly.

Street. She and her former husband John were Harley dealers. "I've had seven Harleys myself, all 1200s. Rode 'em for about fifteen years. The Harleys had too much down time, though; we couldn't seem to keep 'em up. So I went to a Honda; rode it about 30 miles and sold it. I still like that low center of gravity on the Harley-Davidson."

2

On the public morality issue she's sanguine. "Well, they're trying to clamp down on the nudity; there's pros and cons about that. The city is probably losing too much money in fines, that's what a lot of people think. The Buffalo Chip wouldn't let the city police in, said they had their own security. This lawyer that owns it, he's supposed to be quite a character. Lost his beer license. I heard he has it up for sale."

John Klocko, though no longer married to Evelyn, still parks his RV in her front yard. His dealership years included the troubled AMF era. "They were fun, 'course at the time dressers were selling for about $4000. Some years the bikes were terrible. You'd get a worksheet with all the things you were supposed to do before it went on the floor. The reliability is much better now. I had dressers for 13 years, and I was averaging about 15,000 miles a year on 'em. I had bad ones and good ones, but it was fun. I'd fix 'em up and sell 'em and buy a new one.

"They came out with that special Cafe Racer, whenever it was – '76, now that was a super machine. Rode, handled, run like a champ. Why couldn't they build the rest of 'em like that? The quality was there, and the one right along side of it, a dresser or low rider, and it wasn't. We got to the point where we had to take a new machine, strip it all down and take the engine to a machine shop, balance the crank and everything, and man what a difference. I mean you had to spend $1500, but it was terrific."

Evelyn slides in. "I met a gal from Norway, she comes over and buys them. They can't get enough of 'em. They chop 'em over there and all they want are 1200s."

"Well, bucks talk," John says. "Why should they sell it here for $10,000 when they can get $20,000 over there? It's a big thing in Europe and Japan. A prestige thing. I don't blame 'em."

IN THE AFTERNOON the vintage half-mile races are running out at the fairgrounds. Former AMA national racer Neil Keen is hammering his Trackmaster Triumph through the

3

turns, closing on Norm Lehfeldt's BSA. Keen slides through on the last lap to win.

Leonard Schaefer from Fort Calhoun, Nebraska, is racing a '49 Harley flathead. It's making some power, but starts spitting coming off the turns. "I just got this on the track today. Been lookin' for one of these a long time, and I just found it over in Emory, South Dakota. It came out of the barn that way. Didn't do anything but clean the carburetor, except for painting the frame and cleanin' it up."

Does Leonard's wife think 66 might be a little old for this sort of fun? "No, no. We went racing on our honeymoon, in 1951. I raced from '48 to '51, that's when I quit. Sold my bike for $100. We were drinkin' and some guy says I'll give you $100 for it, and I said give it here. I just made up my mind I was gonna quit and raise a family."

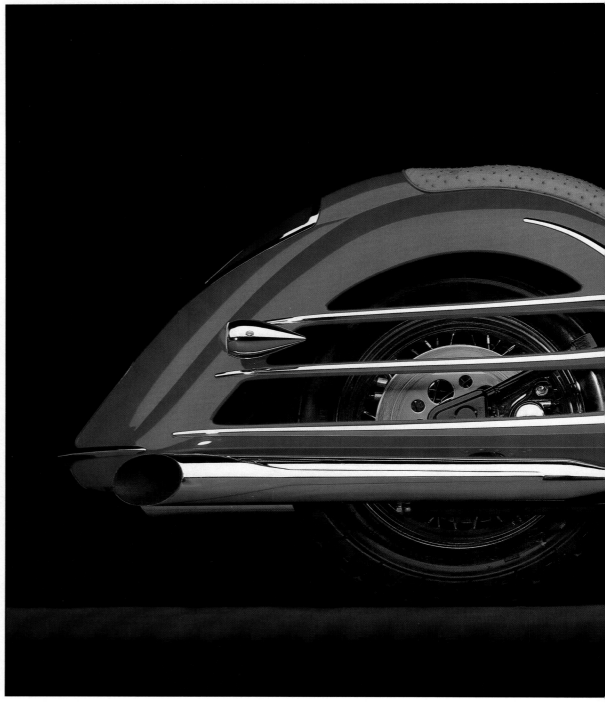

In the pits Wayne Baughman is interviewed by *Easyriders*. Head of the new Indian Motorcycle Manufacturing, Inc., he has the rolling chassis for a 1993 Indian Scout on display. "The engine will have fuel injection and a few other things; it will be a surprise to most people. The engine will be stress tested for 200 hours at redline, just to give you an example that Indian will not do research and development on their customers. People who test the machine will know in an instant that the new 86-cubic-inch, aircooled, all-American V-twin will be an experience they will enjoy. It will be a new thrill, and a new Indian motorcycle for them to ride across this country or around the world if they please.

"The motorcycle is priced competitively. We'll start out with limited production, between 1200 and 2400

The range of decorative styles applied to the Harley-Davidson represents an enormous continuum, the limits of which are set only by the individual imagination. Maybe there are no limits, and the shapes, contours and effects have infinite variety. Maybe only a foundation that changes so little over time is the ideal starting point.

machines in '93. We're taking orders now for start-up delivery in June of 1993. We've had a lot of fun, but the real fun is about to begin. The Indian is back."

Across the highway at the hillclimb, Dave Johston of Billings, Montana, points his Harley at the hill and drops the hammer. The Harley barks loud and devours the 200-foot, double-jump grade in 4.93 seconds. The crowd roars. Boots Weber of Kansas runs second with a 750cc Kawasaki.

Out behind the Super 8 Motel, Chip Coffin is hosing off his Ultra-Classic Electra-Glide with attached trailer, the "H-D Hotel." Chip is a Canadian with a fondness for '49-'51 Mercurys, which he restores and customizes. The trailer was built out of a Hannigan sidecar, weighs 300 pounds and tows easily at high speeds, but sleeps only one. "I took

Bob Dron's Heritage Royale is a machine that seems both classic and futuristic, a design that combines elements of a Bugatti and the Starship *Enterprise*. And yet it's really just a motorcycle, with an ostrich skin seat cover. And it rolls down the road. Ain't life grand?

a trip through California last year, and slept in it 21 of 30 nights." Traveling now with his wife, the trailer is used to stow gear. They're heading off to Branson, Missouri, for the last leg of their vacation.

Riders are headed out as the week draws down, and vendors start to think about packing up. The 50th annual Black Hills Motor Classic drifts toward history, and Sturginians begin thinking about the return to the real world. And 80,000 or so tired, happy, hung-over or well-rested bikers head for the highways. Most will return next year. Because there is, in truth, nothing quite like Sturgis.

HARLEY-DAVIDSON CELEBRATES its 90th anniversary in 1993, marked by three new machines and six limited edition models. The new *Dyna Wide Glide* features Factory Ape Hanger handlebars, tail-light tucked into the bobtail fender, new Fat Bob gas tank and spoked wheels. The Dyna Low Rider has a two-piece seat with a removable passenger section, buckhorn handlebars and dual disc brakes in front. Both models share the Dyna Glide chassis introduced on the '91 Sturgis. The two engine mounts have new support plates and rubber compound for better vibration control.

The 90th Anniversary limited edition trim is available on the 1200 Sportster, Low Rider Custom, Dyna Wide Glide, Electra Glide Classic and Ultra Classic and the Tour Glide Ultra Classic. Each has serialized nameplates, 90th

Anniversary cloisonné tank emblems and two-tone silver/charcoal paint scheme.

The third new model is the Heritage Softail Nostalgia, finished in black and white with matching natural cowhide inserts on the seat and saddlebags. Thus the nickname, "Cow Glide." The Fifties look is enhanced by wide whitewall tires on spoked wheels. The FLSTN is also set for limited production, with only 2700 being produced.

Daytona Beach is like Sturgis with an ocean. Or maybe Sturgis is like Daytona with mountains. Whatever. The gatherings are much the same, though somehow quite different. Folks get a little crazier at Daytona, having been cooped up all winter. The Florida gig has more types of racing, more bikinis and a big beach on which to cruise. What the sites have in common is that each has more Harleys than any other congregation in the known world. Some bikes may resemble a zebra, others can put you in mind of the inside of Uncle Walt's shed down at the farm. And at the Rat's Hole show at the beach, a person can see more sights wonderous and bizarre than the average brain can properly comprehend.

THE LADY RACER

Nancy Delgado was the only woman in the Harley-Davidson Twin Sports series in 1992. The 27-year-old racer from Danbury, Connecticut, is five foot four, weighs 110 pounds, and pilots a 500-pound Sportster on roadracing tracks throughout the country.

"I'd been riding for about a year, and decided to go roadracing because it was a lot less hassle than getting tickets on the street. I started on a Yamaha RD400 and it never finished a race, so I got a Kawasaki EX500 and raced that for a couple years. In 1991 I got my Pro Twins license and did my first pro race at Daytona on a Ducati 650.

"Then I was approached by American Iron magazine, who were interested in someone to write articles about racing a Sportster. Bartels Harley-Davidson came up with the bike and I raced that in '91. Then in '92 Earl Small Harley-Davidson of Atlanta set me up with a ride and I continued writing articles for the magazine. It was difficult the first year at all the nationals, learning all the tracks and being the driver, the racer, the mechanic and the writer. In '92 all I had to do was show up at the race track, but we still didn't have a full-time tuner. Earl Small helped out as much as he could.

"I thought racing Sportsters was going to be a lot worse than it really was. The main problem I had in '91 was the four-speed transmission. I had that thing apart five times. I mean, when you have fear of a bike because it goes into neutral going into a corner, and then it will pop into a gear, any gear, that will slow you down a lot. The five-speed felt so much better. But the bikes handle better than I thought they would. They're good bikes, but you've got to know how to set them up and how to treat them."

1

The new FL series also gets an automotive-style oil pan below the engine, and the battery repositioned below the seat. Larger saddlebags have fixed lids and improved latches.

MILWAUKEE GEARS UP for the 90th Reunion in June '93, with cross-country rides starting from ten points throughout the USA and Canada. The routes will all serve as fundraisers for the Muscular Dystrophy Association, for which Harley-Davidson has raised nearly $11 million dollars in their 11 years as a corporate sponsor. As many as 75,000 riders are expected to converge on Milwaukee.

"We'll have a lot to celebrate in our 90th year," says Harley president Richard F. Teerlink. "During the past ten years, the people of Harley-Davidson have transformed the company from a financially-endangered, below-average quality manufacturer to an industry leader that is now recognized worldwide as a premier manufacturer of superior quality products."

That Harley-Davidson managed to escape the jaws of the conglomerate crusher was a noteworthy achievement; that the company went on to enormous success during an economic recession was remarkable. As former sales director Bill Dutcher says, "Bless their hearts, they pulled out of the death dive and made it. Those people really busted their asses to make it work, starting with Vaughan Beals. They took a hell of a risk and it paid off. Beals has been paid very handsomely, but he risked just about everything he had, and put in Herculean effort and considerable intelligence. I think it's a marvelous business story."

In building modern replicas of its own mid-century machines, Harley-Davidson recreated its own legend. By applying contemporary engineering techniques and manufacturing systems, and retaining its traditional form, the Milwaukee marvel is on the road to its second century of production. The centennial jubilee in 2003 should be some kind of party.

More women are riding motorcycles these days. It might be a Shovelhead springer, Heritage Softail or a racing Sportster. Lots of ladies prefer being at the controls rather than on the back seat. The female flyers also have publications devoted to gender specific coverage of the sport. In the assembly on the right is Linda Giovannoni, Editor of *Harley Women*, to the left, and Courtney Caldwell, Publisher of *American Woman Motorsports*, in the center.

Among the wonderful things about motorcycling, and there are many, is the sense of continuity. Harley-Davidson's history is, in large measure, the story of 20th-century America. The tale now enters its tenth decade. Dramatic and remarkable changes have occurred in ninety years, few more notable than the persistence of The Motor Company of Milwaukee.

The original spirit of this sport abides nowhere more strongly than among the enthusiasts of Harley-Davidson. No other brand owns such a lineage, and today's Harley displays a direct link to its ancestral origins. The faithful vintage flathead, supercharged Evo and twin-carb Knuckle all connect to that unbroken cord running back to 1903, when Bill and Art had a notion for a motorcycle. Four generations and many miles down the road, on the bright California coast, the big smiles affirm continuing faith in the everlasting ride.

TECHNICAL OVERACHIEVEMENT

"There's a certain dynamic that occurs in all enthusiast sports, or at least the two I've been in, where one or two magazines take the lead and the editors write about what's interesting to them. So they propagate this high-end message – technically sophisticated – which leaves the body of the market way behind.

"In windsurfing it has nearly caused the demise of the sport. It's gone from a simple thing in Marina Del Ray, standing on this board and laughing and falling in, to this speed demon thing, which I love, but it leaves the market behind. In motorcycling it was the drag-your-knee/crotch rocket/worship of Kenny Roberts and company. Which I was part of. But when I went to work for Harley I suddenly realized that, wait a minute, there's a whole different thing here. It's going to the park with your friends and grilling some hot dogs, sitting around with your foot up on your bike and listening to each other as humans. Not testing each other's ability to control this dynamic device.

"Windsurfing has done the same thing, and in about one-third the time frame. The question is, if you were God, or the guru of the next enthusiast sport, what would you do? And the answer is – quickly segment out the intellectually elite, including the wannabees, and get them to talk to each other in one corner. And keep the market focused on the basic simplicity and fun in the center of the stage."

Bill Dutcher
All Americade Boy.

The motorcycle remains one of the finest products of the industrial revolution, and the Harley-Davidson stands alone as the machine most representative of motor history. As mechanical folk art it has no equivalent. As a transportation device, the Harley is a fundamental expression of 19th century American steam locomotive power; full-time thrust available on demand, absolutely no waiting. The relaxed pull of smooth, paddlewheel torque, at once effortless and grand.

The origins of motoring freedom are still visible in the profile of a big Milwaukee V-twin. And while a model name like Heritage Nostalgia may ring a little hokey in modern ears, there's no mistaking the appeal. It's in rolling down that sunrise highway, easy thunder at your command; in the wind's own release and the unbound landscape of possibilities, in the roar of the leather, and the smell of the road.

THE SPORTSTERS

IN 1993 THE SPORTSTER was 36 years old, the longest running model in the history of Harley-Davidson. Developed from the flathead K model of the Fifties, the Sporty has a racing history that reaches back to the WR model of the Forties. As the hot rod of the Harley line, the XL is lighter and faster than the big twins, making it the natural choice for racing. The XR750 competition engine was developed from the Sportster, and is still the dominant force in dirt track racing.

The versatility of the Sportster has been shown by the wide range of competition categories in which it is found. Whether it's dirt track, roadracing or drag racing, Sportsters are built by committed enthusiasts to do the job.

In roadracing, the Harley-Davidson Twin Sport series has pushed development into new realms in terms of both power and handling. The series has proven popular with amateur racers operating under the restrictions of limited funds. Harley fans are hoping the new 883 dirt track series will have the same result. The Sportster continues to be a favorite of drag racers as well. Novice racers will appreciate the *Sportster Performance Handbook*, by Buzz Buzzelli.

THE DYNA GLIDES

THE CHASSIS FOR THE DYNA GLIDE series was the first computer-aided design in the Harley line-up. It first appeared in 1991 as the basis for the Sturgis model, and employs a two-point rubber engine isolation mounting system. The oil tank is mounted below the transmission. Both Dyna Glide models have five-speed transmissions and belt drive.

The Wide Glide styling evolved from a model of the same name first produced in 1980. The newest version wears Factory Ape Hanger handlebars, spoked wheels and a bobtail rear fender. The forward mounted footpegs contribute to the laid back riding position.

The Low Rider has lower bars and cast wheels with dual disc brakes at the front. The passenger seat is removable. Both Dyna Glides have a 1340cc engine.

THE LOW RIDERS

THE FXR SERIES CAN be traced back to the Super Glide of 1971. Designed to fill the gap between the Sportster and the Electra Glide, the original FX generated a five-model roster of trim heavyweights with a range of custom and sport features.

The Low Rider and Super Glide both have low seat heights that appeal to shorter riders, and use buckhorn handlebars. The Sport Glide is equipped with half-fairing, saddlebags, passenger back rest and dual front disc brakes.

The Low Rider Sport carries a longer fork and shocks for improved ground clearance and better handling in the twisties. It wears lower handlebars and is fitted with an air-adjustable front suspension. The Convertible has the same features, plus a backrest, Lexan windshield and removable saddlebags. All Low Riders have rubber-mounted 1340cc engines, five-speeds and belt drive.

The Low Riders have been the most well received H-D models in recent years. In terms of custom fitting the right combination of style and performance to individual tastes, the FXR series has established a comprehensive rider base.

With sufficient size and power for the open road, yet agile enough for use in town and on back roads, the Low Riders appeal to commuters, sport riders and all-around enthusiasts who appreciate an all-purpose machine. Many women have begun on Sportsters and moved to the Low Rider for the added smoothness and comfort.

THE FL TOURING SERIES

THE HARLEY-DAVIDSON TOURING BIKES are all equipped with air-adjustable front and rear suspension, rider and passenger footboards and saddlebags. All have 1340cc engine with five-speed transmission and belt drive. The Electra Glide Sport has an adjustable Lexan windshield and is designed as a sport-touring heavyweight.

The Electra Glide Classic has a fork-mounted fairing and an AM/FM/cassette stereo system. The Ultra Classic has a four-speaker stero, CB/voice-activated intercom and helmet-mounted headset.

The Tour Glide Ultra Classic features a frame-mounted fairing, higher bars and different seating position. All models have below-engine oil pans, below-seat batteries, adjustable footboards and hinged saddlebags.

THE SOFTAIL SERIES

THE STYLING EMPHASIS of the Softail series represents the design elements of motorcycles from the past. The FX models use 21-inch front wheels and more modern styling, while the FL versions evoke an older era. The Fat Boy and Heritage Softail Nostalgia are two variations on the historical theme. The disc wheels, sculptured fender and shotgun-style exhaust system set the Fat Boy apart. The Nostalgia runs whitewall tires on spoked wheels, and a black-and-white paint scheme.

The Softails have found a niche among riders looking for a stylish machine that also has the necessary creature comforts. These are the neo-classic cruisers of the Nineties, with a range of graphic choices. Bikes that look like the Old Days but perform like today.

187

The Springer Softail uses the style of the 1948 girder/spring fork to establish a traditional profile. The addition of a central shock absorber brings roadholding up to modern standards. The Softail Custom also uses a spoked 21-inch front wheel and a 16 in the back. The Fat Bob fuel tank and padded backrest are favored cruiser pieces. The Softail Classic's fat tires and full fenders recall the mellow Fifties, embellished by the studded seat and fishtail mufflers.

THE MILWAUKEE MILESTONES

1902 William S. Harley and Arthur Davidson complete the first actual Harley-Davidson engine, its 3-inch bore and 3-1/2 stroke producing three horsepower. Arthur's brother, Walter Davidson, had returned from Kansas for the wedding of the third brother, William. When Walter, a machinist, and William Davidson, a toolmaker, join the team, the Harley-Davidson Motor Company is on the road.

1903 The first Harley-Davidson production motorcycle is made, followed by two more. Each single-cylinder, belt-drive machine has been sold in advance. According to the company history, the first machine went to a Mr. Meyer, who logged 6,000 miles before selling it. The ensuing four owners added 77,000 miles to the original bike. In 1913 the factory claimed that No. 1 was still on the road, with the original bearings, and had traveled more than 100,000 miles.

1904 Production again totals 3 machines, now nicknamed the Silent Gray Fellow. The conservative color and quiet muffler indicate Milwaukee's interest in social acceptance for the new machines.

1905 The first outside employee is hired and production rises to seven units.

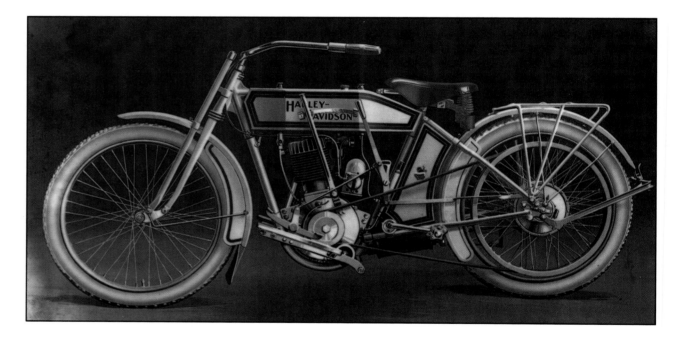

Engines are available separately for the first time, and carburetors, boat motors and propellers are added to the sales catalog.

1906 A Davidson uncle, James McLay, finances construction of a new plant on the site that becomes Harley-Davidson's permanent location. The Juneau Avenue factory adds five more employees and production increases to 50 motorcycles. William Harley takes a leave of absence to study engineering at the University of Wisconsin.

Motorcycling in 1913 was a considerably more challenging proposition than it is today.

1907 Harley-Davidson becomes a corporation, with shares divided among 17 employees. Total production rises to 150 machines, among them the first sold for use by the police.

1908 A prototype of the first 1000cc V-twin wins a hillclimb in Algonquin, Illinois. More factory space is added and overall production climbs to 410. Walter Davidson wins the 365-mile

Federation of American Motorcyclists endurance run in New York with a perfect score

1909 The 7-horsepower, 45-degree V-twin is produced to compete with the popular Indian. Valve train design proves inadequate, and the twin is withdrawn for more development.

1911 The twin is reintroduced with mechanical valves and a new frame. Belt drive remains standard.

1912 The V-twin gets chain drive and a rear wheel clutch. The Full-Floating Seat, designed by Bill Harley, features center post suspension. Seven people die at a New Jersey motordrome racing accident.

1913 A new 5-horsepower, 35 cubic inch single is offered with belt or chain drive. Also new is a two-speed rear hub. William Ottaway, formerly of Thor Motorcycles, is hired as manger of the new H-D racing team.

1914 The kickstarter and internal expanding rear brake are new features. Volume sales are made to the U.S. Army and postal service.

1915 Improvements include a 3-speed transmission and engine clutch. Otto Walker and Red Parkhurst, of the Harley Wrecking Crew, finish 1-2 in the 300-mile race at Venice, California. The delivery side-van debuts.

1916 Milwaukee offers kitted 11-horsepower V-twins for racing at $250. Military sidecars are equipped with machine gun mounts for use on the Mexican border and the war in Europe.

1917 The U.S. enters the war and H-D converts to military production. The factory service school is established to train mechanics for the war effort. Milwaukee enters the bicycle market.

1918 World War I ends in November. Dispatch rider Roy Holtz, of Chippewa Falls, Wisconsin, is the first American to enter Germany.

1919 H-D introduces the 600cc model W, a horizontally opposed sport twin.

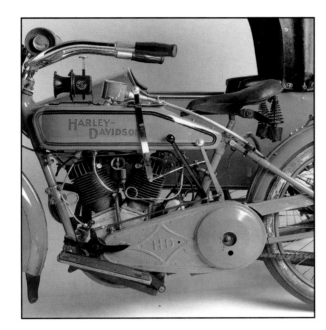

By 1918 there were twice the cylinders and power enough to pull a sidecar and a pal.

Unlike any Harley before or since, the model was unsuccessful and was discontinued after four years. Overall production in Milwaukee rose to more than 22,000 motorcycles and 16,000 sidecars.

1920 Team rider Red Parkhurst sets new speed records at Daytona Beach, Florida. Mass production of cars depresses motorcycle sales. H-D begins new ad campaign to counteract negative public image of motorcycles. Harley dealerships exist in 67 countries around the world.

1921 H-D production drops to 10,000 machines. Sidecars get increased emphasis in company advertising.

1922 The 1200cc side-valve F model V-twin appears, rated at 18 horsepower. Military olive green replaced by brighter green with gold striping. Harley ads focus on growing number of woman riders.

1923 Factory racing team discontinued. The company catalog of clothing and accessories gets new emphasis, as does an aggressive financing plan.

1925 The teardrop fuel tank is part of the "Stream-Line" models, offered at reduced prices. A new 500cc side-valve single is added to the line.

1929 The second generation of Davidsons, and a Harley, join the firm. The 750cc side-valve V-twin WL model debuts at $290. The new twin-cam 1200cc twin is $370. The Great Depression descends.

1930 Removable Ricardo cylinder heads for twins and singles, plus larger brakes and dual beam headlights. Bill Davidson, son of company VP, wins the 420-mile Jack Pine Tour in Michigan.

1931 The 3-wheeled Servi-Car appears and commercial markets grow in importance.

1933 Depression deepens; Milwaukee cuts back to two-day work week.

1935 Harley racer Joe Petrali wins every national dirt track race of the year. Milwaukee displays new 1000cc OHV Knucklehead and 1340cc side-valve for 1936.

1937 Joe Petrali rides the Knucklehead to new speed record of 136 mph at Daytona. Founder William A. Davidson dies at age 66.

1940 The 750, 1200 and 1340cc engines get aluminum heads. More military versions of 750 shipped to England and Russia. The 1200cc OHV FL model readied for release in '41.

This fine 1943 WL is owned by Joe Callahan of Highland, Michigan. Wave if you see him!

1941 Civilian production ceases at year's end; U.S. enters World War II. H-D builds nearly 90,000 WLA models for the military. BMW-style shaft-drive

The 1941 Knucklehead was one muscular looking machine. Owner: Marty Beaulieu.

opposed twin, model XA, developed for desert warfare; only 1000 made.

1942 Company President Walter Davidson dies, followed the next year by William Harley. Only Arthur Davidson remains of the founding four.

1947 Full civilian production resumes with updated '41 models. Accessories and clothing catalog grows larger; first appearance of zippered black leather jacket. Motorcycle gangs get increasing publicity.

1948 The Hummer debuts, a 125cc two-stroke based on DKW design. The big twins get hydraulic lifters, and the Knucklehead is discontinued in favor of the new 1200cc Panhead. Production numbers rise significantly.

1949 The Hydra-Glide arrives, an FL with telescopic fork and deeply valanced fenders.

1950 Arthur Davidson, 69, and his wife die in an automobile accident.

1952 The K model, a 750cc side-valve V-twin, replaces the venerable WL. Unit construction gears, hand clutch and footshift making the racing KR model an instant success.

1953 Milwaukee celebrates 50th anniversary. The 125cc grows to 165.

1954 The K model becomes the KH at 55 cubic inches, forerunner to the Sportster.

1956 Leroy Winters wins Jack Pine on a 165. Elvis Presley buys a red and white KH model.

1957 The KH becomes the XL Sportster with overhead valves.

1958 The FL evolves as the Duo-Glide with swingarm suspension and hydraulic rear brake. The Sportster gets more horsepower.

1959 Carroll Resweber wins second of four straight national racing titles for H-D. Honda 50cc mini-bikes appear in USA.

1960 Milwaukee buys half interest in Aermacchi of Italy and imports the Sprint, a 250cc 4-stroke single. Harley KR riders sweep top 14 places in the Daytona 200.

1963 William G. Davidson, eldest son of William H., joins the company as director of styling.

1965 Roger Reiman sets 250cc Bonneville record of 177 mph in a Sprint- powered streamliner. H-D markets a 50cc Aermacchi for $225.

1966 The Duo-Glide gets electric start and becomes Electra Glide, known as the Shovelhead. New cams and carburetor give the Sportster more grunt, and electric start for '67.

1968 Cal Rayborn rides KR to Daytona victory, first to average more than 100 mph.

1969 Rayborn repeats at Daytona. Harley-Davidson sold to conglomerate American Machine and Foundry (AMF).

1970 Rayborn sets world record of 265 mph at Bonneville in Sportster-powered streamliner. KR replaced by XR-750 developed by Dick O'Brien.

Dave Royal's 1936 80-cubic-inch (1340cc) VLH flathead was only made during one year and was silver and green.

1971 AMF logo added to gas tanks. FX1200 Super Glide debuts, a Willie G. design. Evel Knievel jumps to fame.

1972 Sportster grows to 1000cc. Mark Brelsford regains national title on XR-750. Electra Glide gets front disc brake.

As indicated by the faired fork, vertical handlebars, tank pad and slick tires, the Tramp was built to go very straight and fast.

1978 Electra Glide grows to 1340cc. H-D celebrates 75th birthday.

1979 Two-stroke production discontinued. Willie G. offers limited edition Electra Glide Classic with sidecar. AMF looks to sell Harley-Davidson.

1980 The FLT Tour Glide and Wide Glide factory custom premier, and the FXB Sturgis with belt drive.

1986 H-D contributes $250,000 for Statue of Liberty renovation. The Sportster 883cc Evolution debuts, at $3995. The FL Heritage Softail blends new technology with 50s look. Company goes public with 2 million shares of common stock. H-D acquires Holiday Rambler,

1987 Electra Glide Sport, Heritage Softail Classic and Low Rider Custom are unveiled, and 30th Anniversary 1100cc Sportster. President Reagan visits York plant. H-D listed on New York Stock Exchange.

1988 Sportster grows to 1200cc. Springer Softail celebrates 85th anniversary. Milwaukee festivities raise $600,000 for Muscular Dystrophy Association.

1990 The FLSTF Fat Boy appears, another Willie G. retro-style. New Dyna Glide Sturgis shown at 50th Black Hills Classic in Sturgis, South Dakota. Attendance reaches 250,000-plus.

1991 Sportsters get 5-speeds and belt drive. Scott Parker wins fourth Grand National title in a row, equalling Carroll Resweber's feat. HOG chapters reach 650 worldwide.

1992 The FX Daytona and Custom models get new Dyna Glide frame, Sportster Hugger features lower ride height. Chris Carr wins Grand National Championship.

1993 New Dyna Wide Glide has factory Ape Hanger handlebars. Heritage Softail Nostalgia has cowhide inserts on seat and bags. Limited editions of Sportster, Low Rider, Wide-, Electra-, and Tour Glide commemorate H-D 90th anniversary. Milwaukee hosts huge birthday party.

2003 [Projected] The Hog turns 100. Harley-Davidson Centennial Celebration declared national holiday. Washington, D.C. party attracts two million bikers. Donations erase national debt. President Bill Bradley appoints Willie G. Davidson Director of Transportation.

1973 Assembly operations moved from Milwaukee to AMF plant in York, Pennsylvania. William H. Davidson retires.

1975 The Sprint is dropped. Walter Villa wins second of three consecutive world roadracing titles on Aermacchi RR-250.

1976 Relations deteriorate between H-D management, labor and AMF directors. Quality control suffers. H-D releases Liberty Editions to mark USA bicentennial.

1977 Willie G. presents the Sportster-based XLCR Cafe Racer and FXS Low Rider version of Super Glide. Jay Springsteen wins first of three Grand National titles on XR-750.

1981 H-D managers, led by AMF executive Vaughan Beals, purchase Harley from AMF in leveraged buy-out.

1982 President Ronald Reagan grants H-D relief from imported competition, puts 45% tariff on Japanese heavyweight machines. FXR Super Glide II gets rubber-mount engine, 5-speed.

1983 Harley Owners Group (H.O.G.) inaugurated. H-D legal dept. goes after trademark infringers. FXRT sport tourer gets air fork and computer controlled ignition.

1984 Introduction of 1340cc Evolution engine, and XR-1000 Sportster. The FX Softail debuts. H-D regains California Highway Patrol contract.

Bronze sculpture by Steve Posson.

PICTURE CREDITS

Contents page, clockwise from top right: Dewhurst, Tod Rafferty, Tod Rafferty, Michael Lichter/*Easyriders*, Neil A. Miller, James Schnepf, Dewhurst, Dewhurst, Dewhurst, Tria Giovan, Tria Giovan, Tria Giovan, Milwaukee County Historical Society, Milwaukee County Historical Society;
© **Bill Ashe Studio**: pages 108-109, 146;
© **Dewhurst Photography**: back of jacket, title page, pages 45 (right), 133 (bottom), 136, 137, 138, 139, 145 (top), 148-49, 154-55, 155, 158, 163, 174, 176, 176-77, 191;
Tria Giovan, © CLB: pages 43 (left), 44, 48, 49, 58, 58-59, 62, 63, 64 (top left), 74, 75, 76 (top), 88-89, 89, 156 (bottom), 157, 190 (bottom);
David Goldman, © **Roland Brown:** pages 172-73;
Grubman, © CLB: pages 12-13, 16 (top), 16-17, 26-27, 46, 46-47, 50 (top), 50-51, 52 (top), 52-53, 56-57, 57, 59 (bottom), 60-61, 62-63, 64 (top right), 64-65, 65 (top), 66, 66-67, 67, 68-69, 70-71, 71, 72, 72-73, 74-75, 76-77, 79 (bottom), 80-81, 82 (top), 82-83, 85 (top), 86-87, 90-91, 92, 93 (top), 96-97, 98, 98-99 (top and bottom), 102-103, 106-107, 117 (top), 118-19, 162-63, 189, 190 (top);
© **Ron Kimball**: front of jacket, pages 174-75;
© **Michael Lichter/***Easyriders***: pages 4, 6-7, 9 (right), 18-19, 22, 23 (top), 29 (top), 30, 31 (top), 34 (top), 35, 38-39, 40, 41 (top), 42-43, 47, 54, 55, 78, 79 (top), 84-85, 85 (bottom), 94 (left), 100-101, 101, 112-13, 114-15, 121,122-23, 128-29, 130, 131 (bottom right), 132-33,136-37, 142-43, 143, 144-45, 147 (bottom), 150, 150-51, 151, 156 (top), 166-67, 167, 168-69, 180 (bottom), 190 (top);
© **Neil A. Miller**: pages 95 (top), 103 (top), 104, 105, 164 (bottom right);
Courtesy of Milwaukee Co. Historical Society: pages 8, 9 (left), 10, 11 (bottom), 12 (top), 14, 15 (top and center), 16 (bottom), 20-21, 21, 23 (bottom), 24, 25, 26, 28, 29 (bottom), 31 (bottom), 32, 32-33, 33, 34 (bottom), 36 (top), 37, 41 (bottom), 188;
© **Brian J. Nelson**: page 178;
Photofest: pages 93 (bottom), 94 (top right and center), 95 (bottom), 147 (center);
© **Tod Rafferty**: pages 15 (bottom), 110, 113, 115, 124-25, 126, 127 (top left and right), 131 (bottom left), 133 (top), 140, 140-41, 141, 152, 153, 159, 168, 170-71, 171, 173, 175 (bottom), 178, 180 (top), 192;
© **James Schnepf**: half-title page, pages 11 (top), 36 (bottom), 53, 111, 116, 117 (bottom), 120, 125, 127 (bottom), 129 (top right), 131 (top), 134-35, 145 (bottom), 147 (top), 148, 149, 160, 161, 164 (top and bottom left), 165, 170 (bottom), 179, 181;

The Publishers would like to thank the following for kindly allowing their bikes to be photographed:
Jim Allen, Marty Beaulieu, Robert Beenenga, Ron Bergan, Tom Boyer, J.F. Burkhalten, Joe Callahan, Jerry Christensen, Don Cox, Richard Davies, Jack Dillingham, Greg Duray, Don Fiedler, Ben Griffith, Brian Haenlien, Henny Harrison, Hershel Jones, Les Joseph, Jim Kersting, Steve Ketchum, Dave Kurth, W.P. Leedom, Butch Lightweight, Bruce Lindsay, Bob McClean, Rob Maertz, Ron Magers, Joe Martin, Bill Mathis, Kevin Meyer, Mike Millay, Raymond Miller, Moon Mullins, Doug Murray, Mike Novak, Tami Ortner, Jerry Parmenter, Bob Pease, Edmond Porras, John Rank, Dave Royal, Robert D. Saar, Ken Schneider, Bob Shirey, Mark Smith, Mike Smith, Rudy and Anna Solis, Tony Stewart, Bob Southwick, Darin Taylor, Kenny Thomas, Chuck Todd, Stanley Waite, Tony Watson, Paul Wheeler, George Wills, Scott Yates.

Special thanks to the Tom Kowalski Collection, Denver, Colorado.
Thanks to Jimmie Ditzel and Tom Simmons.